The Adult Years:
Continuity and Change

Master Lecturers

Paul T. Costa, Jr.
Margaret Gatz
Bernice L. Neugarten
Timothy A. Salthouse
Ilene C. Siegler

Edited by
Martha Storandt
and Gary R. VandenBos

AMERICAN PSYCHOLOGICAL ASSOCIATION
WASHINGTON, DC 20036

Library of Congress Cataloging-in-Publication Data

The Adult years.

(The Master lectures; v. 8)
Contents: Age-related changes in basic cognitive processes /
Timothy A. Salthouse—Personality continuity and the changes of
adult life / Paul T. Costa, Jr.—Clinical psychology and aging /
Margaret Gatz—[etc.]
1. Aging—Psychological aspects. 2. Adulthood—Psycho-
logical aspects. 3. Aged—Psychology. I. Storandt, Martha. II.
VandenBos, Gary R. III. American Psychological Association. IV.
Series.
BF724.55.A35A35   1989   155.6   89-6992
ISBN 1-55798-061-6

First Printing July 1989
Second Printing October 1991

Copies may be ordered from:
Order Department, P.O. Box 2710
Hyattsville, MD 20784

Published by the American Psychological Association, Inc.
1200 Seventeenth Street, N.W., Washington, DC 20036
Copyright © 1989 by the American Psychological Association.

Printed in the United States of America.

CONTENTS

MASTER LECTURES

Self-Study Program

The Master Lectures Self-Study Program provides an opportunity for individuals to earn Category I Continuing Education Credit for reading this and other Master Lectures volumes. The Self-Study Program consists of a multiple-choice test developed to accompany each volume of this series, beginning with Volume 2; up to 10 CE Credits per volume may be earned. For further information about the Master Lectures Self-Study Program (ML-SSP), please write or phone:

APA Continuing Education Program
Attention: ML-SSP
1200 Seventeenth Street, N.W.
Washington, DC 20036
(703) 247-7880

PREFACE

The chapters in this book are based on the Master Lectures given at the annual convention of the American Psychological Association in August 1988. The purpose of the APA Master Lectures is to provide a state-of-the-art review of advances in knowledge, focusing each year on a different topic. These reviews are designed primarily for practitioners and teachers of psychology.

The choice of adulthood and aging as the subject for the 1988 Master Lectures reflects the Continuing Education Committee's recognition that ours is an aging society. The baby-boom generation is now entering middle age and is only two decades away from the retirement years. The fastest-growing segment of our population consists of those over age 85. Not only are the numbers of older people increasing, but people are living longer today than ever before. This means that those requiring psychological services are increasingly likely to be older. Psychologists need to be prepared to meet these needs.

Part of this preparation involves training greater numbers of geropsychologists for both practice and research. This issue was the focus of the 1981 "Older Boulder" national training conference on meeting the mental health needs of older adults. In addition to the necessity for more specialists in gerontological psychology, there is a need for psychologists in all specialties to consider how they might serve the needs of the older population. The Older Boulder conference recommended that teachers of psychology incorporate material on adulthood and aging into all their courses. (The activities of the Older Boulder conference are reported in *Psychology and the Older Adult*, edited by John F. Santos and Gary R. VandenBos, APA, 1982.)

The psychologist who works with older clients must be more of a generalist than those who specialize in working with other age groups. Aging is a biological, psychological, and social process. Frequently it is not possible to address a psychological problem in isolation. For example, aging is associated with an increase in physical illness. To meet the needs of older adults, the clinical psychologist must attend to both mental and physical health concerns, as well as their interaction. Similarly, it is necessary to consider the social context of an older client. Housing, transportation, or economic concerns may play a major role in the client's psychological distress. Thus, the psychologist who has older clients must often look beyond his or her own skills to seek support and advice from professionals of other disciplines. To do this, the psychologist must learn the vocabularies of other health professions well enough to make communication possible. Serving the client effectively also requires putting aside traditional battles. This is easier for gerontological psychologists than for practitioners in most other areas because colleagues in geriatric medicine, nursing, and social work also are aware that aging is a biopsychosocial phenomenon.

The older patient is much less likely to be treated solely as an individual. Often the practitioner must consider a spouse or other family members, such as adult children or the client's siblings. It may be that neighbors or friends are significant others in the older adult's social and psychological world. In some instances, such as with clients in nursing homes, staff must also be considered as part of the "family" system.

The practitioner who works with older adults is often confronted with the need to differentiate between normal age-related declines (and the limitations associated with them) and pathological conditions. This is the case especially with respect to cognitive problems: Are the memory difficulties reported by the client normal for age, or do they indicate mild dementia? Do reduced appetite, sleep difficulties, and fatigue indicate depression, or are they part of "normal" aging? The gerontological practitioner must know about health as well as illness, about normality as well as abnormality.

The chapters in this book provide an introduction to our knowledge about adulthood and aging. Timothy Salthouse and Paul T. Costa, Jr. review what is known about normal aging with respect to cognition and personality, respectively. Margaret Gatz's chapter includes a casebook that provides excellent examples of typical older clients and the problems they face. Ilene Siegler describes the important interface with health psychology. Bernice Neugarten addresses the social context, especially in terms of social policy as it relates to the older population.

There are a number of other sources that can be consulted. The American Psychological Association's 1986 *Handbook of Clinical Memory Assessment*, edited by Leonard Poon, is now in its second printing. A chapter by Powell Lawton and Martha Storandt in McReynolds and Chelune's *Advances in Psychological Assessment*, 6th ed. (Jossey-Bass, 1984) provides a survey of assessment procedures appropriate for older adults. John Herr and John Weakland's *Counseling Elders and Their Families: Practical Techniques for Applied Gerontology* (Springer, 1979) is a classic and is as appropriate today as it was when first published. Bob Knight's *Psychotherapy with Older Adults* (Sage, 1985) is based on his years of experience working with older adults at a community mental health center. Richard Hussian and Ronald Davis's *Responsive Care: Behavioral Interventions with Elderly Persons* (Res Press, 1985) describes the application of a wide range of behavioral techniques to the problems experienced by older individuals. Robert Butler and Myrna Lewis's *Aging and Mental Health: Positive Psychosocial and Biomedical Approaches*, 3rd ed. (Merrill, 1982) contains an excellent chapter on drug therapies and the special problems that exist in pharmaceutical treatments of older adults.

These are just a few of the numerous chapters and books that have appeared in the 10 years since the last Master Lectures on aging, when Powell Lawton, in his lecture on the clinical psychology of aging, bemoaned the lack of attention to this area. Other examples of increased activity can be found in APA's new journal, *Psychology and Aging*, which includes the latest in research on assessment and treatment of older adults.

Practice with older clients is a new and growing opportunity for psychologists. In addition to the increasing numbers of young professionals who have the foresight to recognize the exciting and rewarding challenges presented in working with older people, this field may be especially attractive also to psychologists now in their middle and later years, who are experiencing their own aging. Developing a new area of expertise is a sure way for these practitioners to add zest and vigor to their professional lives.

Martha Storandt
Gary R. VandenBos

TIMOTHY A. SALTHOUSE

AGE-RELATED CHANGES IN BASIC COGNITIVE PROCESSES

Timothy A. Salthouse, currently a professor of psychology at the Georgia Institute of Technology in Atlanta, has had a distinguished career in the field of gerontology and geriatrics. After receiving a PhD in experimental psychology from the University of Michigan, he was awarded a postdoctoral research fellowship in the Aging and Development Program, Department of Psychology, Washington University, St. Louis. Following that appointment, he was affiliated with the Psychology Department at the University of Missouri, progressing from an assistant professor to a full professor during his 10-year stay. In 1982–1983, he was a fellow of the Andrew Norman Institute for Advanced Study in Gerontology and Geriatrics in Los Angeles, and in 1985 and 1987, he was selected Visiting Scientist at the Max Planck Institute for Human Development and Education in West Berlin, Federal Republic of Germany.

In addition to serving as a member of the editorial boards of three major journals in the field of gerontology and aging, as well as associate editor of the second and third editions of the *Handbook of the Psychology of Aging*, Salthouse has been a reviewer for numerous journals, the National Institutes of Aging and of Education, the Veterans Administration, the American Psychological Association (APA), and the National Science Foundation. He has authored 2 books, 14 chapters, and approximately 30 articles on aging and cognition. Salthouse is an APA member and a Fellow of Divisions 3 (Experimental Psychology) and 20

(Adult Development and Aging). He is also a member of the American Association for the Advancement of Science, the Gerontological Society, and the Psychonomic Society.

AGE-RELATED CHANGES IN BASIC COGNITIVE PROCESSES

Controversy Over Cognitive Decline

The topic of changes in basic cognitive processes across the adult years has been the focus of considerable controversy within the field of psychology of aging. A primary goal of this chapter is to describe the major issues involved in this controversy and to summarize some of the empirical evidence relevant to those issues. The presentation is organized in three sections. The first is a discussion of the historical background of research on the relation between age and cognitive processes; this history documents the phenomena of interest and provides a brief chronology to help place the contributions in their appropriate temporal context. The second section focuses on distinctions between the processes found to change with increased age and those that seem to be independent of age-related changes. The final section is devoted to examining evidence relevant to several of the hypotheses that have been proposed to account for the phenomenon of age-related decline in cognitive functioning.

Because the title of this chapter includes the phrase "basic cognitive processes," it is useful to begin by briefly describing what is meant by this term. For the present purposes, basic cognitive processes are what are measured in subtests of batteries that are designed to assess intellectual or neuropsychological status, in a variety of experimental cognitive tasks. This is clearly an atheoretical definition, but it does serve to distinguish the presumably elementary aspects of cognition that have received the most attention by psychological researchers from the more complex aspects of cognition involved in academic, occupational, and artistic achievements. An assumption implicit in much of the research on basic cognitive processes is that complex cognition will eventually be understood in terms of basic cognitive processes. Because few efforts to date have actually focused on the decomposition of complex cognition, however, this discussion will be restricted to relatively basic cognitive processes.

It is important to mention at the outset that this survey of research on age-related changes in basic cognitive processes is prejudiced in favor of studies that have the largest samples of research participants. There are two reasons for using studies that have this bias. One is simply to provide the best possible information about the relation between age and basic cognitive processes, and the best data are usually derived from the largest samples. A second reason is that such samples frequently include people from throughout the entire adult age range, thus allowing examination of the complete function relating cognitive performance to adult age.

This latter information is valuable because one controversial issue associated with the topic of age-related differences in cognition has been ascertaining when age-related cognitive decline first begins. That is, some researchers (e.g., Labouvie-Vief & Chandler, 1978; Schaie, 1979) have suggested that age-related cognitive decline is not noticeable until the postretirement years of the late 60s, whereas others (e.g., Welford, 1966) have claimed that the decline is continuous starting from the mid- to late 20s.

It is interesting to consider why there might be controversy about what is presumably an objective characteristic of a phenomenon, namely, when the function relating chronological age to cognitive performance first begins to decline. Some of these differences in opinion probably originate because different sets of data were being considered, and, as will be seen, the age trends do vary across different measures of cognition. There can also be divergence of opinion concerning exactly the same data, however, because of the various ways in which the question of when decline first occurs can be interpreted. For example, one may interpret the question in terms of where the first perceptible difference occurs. That is, one might imagine a horizontal line across the peak of the age–performance function and then identify decline as occurring at the age when the first gap is apparent between that horizontal line and the function relating age to performance.

A second method of identifying when decline first occurs is to determine the youngest age at which there is a statistically significant difference from the age of peak performance. Determining when the difference from peak performance first exceeds some population-referenced criterion, such as one standard deviation, or less than 50-percent overlap with the reference group at peak performance, is another means of determining when age-related decline occurs. Finally, declines might be identified when differences are detected by any of the previous methods across a specified measurement interval, such as 5 or 10 years.

Although precise conclusions may not be justified, many of the methodological disputes concerning the question of when decline first occurs can be avoided if researchers examine complete age functions. That is, although it may not be feasible to be specific about the exact age at which change is first evident, when data are available from the entire adult age range it is at least possible to examine the general relation between age and cognitive performance, and thus informally evaluate the suggestion that cognitive decline does not occur until the period of late adulthood.

A History of the Research

One of the first large-scale investigations of adult age differences was conducted in Galton's anthropometric laboratory in the International Health Exhibition in 1884 and reported by Koga and Morant (1923). Galton's study was unique in several respects. First, unlike most contemporary studies in which researchers feel obliged to pay, or otherwise compensate, people for participating in their research projects, Galton actually charged participants a nominal fee for the privilege of contributing data to his project. This was apparently not a deterrent in the recruiting of potential participants, because more than 9,000 individuals contributed data to the study, and the resulting data set is still one of the largest concerned with age-related individual differences.

A second unique aspect of Galton's study was that the focus was on physical characteristics rather than mental characteristics. Actually it is somewhat misleading to claim that Galton did not measure mental characteristics, because according to the associationist theories of his time, an individual's mental or cognitive power was reflected in his or her sensory acuity and quickness of response. That is, the number of ideas available to a person was assumed to be partially determined by the ability to register sensations, and the formation of complex thoughts or higher-order ideas was postulated to be influenced by the speed of association.

Results from two of the tasks employed by Galton, consisting of the measurement of auditory frequency sensitivity and simple reaction time, are displayed in Figure 1. It is interesting to note that whereas the age trend is unmistakable in the case of the highest audible pitch, only a very slight trend is evident with the measure of simple reaction time. More recent studies have more profound effects of age in reaction time

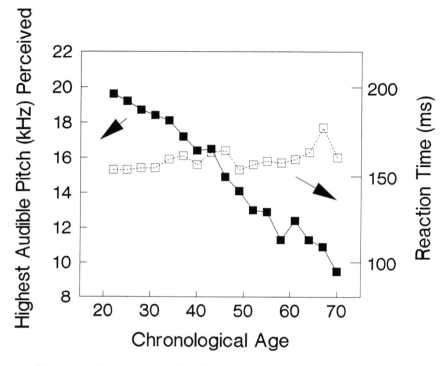

Figure 1. Measurement of auditory sensitivity and simple reaction time according to age. Data from Galton's anthropometric laboratory and reported by Koga and Morant (1923).

measures, and it is possible that Galton's reaction time data may have been unreliable because of the combination of a potentially imprecise pendulum chronoscope and the availability of only a few measurements from each individual.

The entry of the United States into World War I provided the impetus for the development of the first group-administered intelligence test designed for adults. This test, the Army Alpha, was in many respects the prototype of adult intelligence tests because it consisted of a battery of eight subtests similar to those still used in contemporary intelligence batteries. For example, among the subtests included were arithmetic reasoning, which consisted of arithmetic word problems; number series completion, in which the examinee was to complete a numerical sequence; verbal analogies, which required the selection of a word that had the same relation to a target word as the relation evident in two other words; and a synonym–antonym vocabulary test.

A total of more than 1.75 million soldiers were eventually tested with either the Army Alpha test or the nonverbal Army Beta test. Results from more than 15,000 officers tested with the Army Alpha are illustrated in Figure 2. The data in this figure are based on the sum of the scores across the eight subtests. The summed scores were converted to a relative scale according to this method: The mean at each age was divided by the maximum score across all ages. A clear trend for these percentage-of-the-maximum values to decrease more or less continuously beginning at about age 25 is obvious.

One of the concerns raised about the Army data was that the age trends might have been spurious because of unrepresentative samples of middle-aged adults in the military. That is, although the young officers might have been representative of the general population, it was hypothesized that many of the most intelligent men in their 30s, 40s, and 50s might have been exempted from military service because they were successfully engaged in essential civilian occupations.

Jones and Conrad, in a study published in 1933, provided data relevant to the question of whether an artifact of unrepresentative

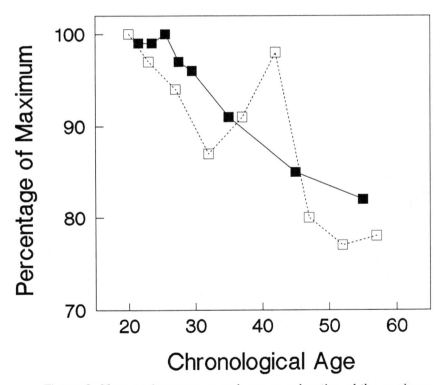

Figure 2. Mean performance at each age as a function of the maximum performance across all ages on the Army Group Examination Alpha intelligence battery. The Army data (■) are derived from Yerkes (1921), and the New England data (□) are derived from Jones and Conrad (1933).

sampling was responsible for the decline in performance with increased age that was observed in the Army data. These researchers avoided the problem of differential representativeness by administering the Army Alpha to nearly the entire adult population of several rural New England communities. The results from their study are also illustrated in Figure 2. These data are noisier than the Army data, perhaps because of the much smaller sample (i.e., only 678 people, compared with 15,385 in the Army sample). Nevertheless, with the exception of the anomalous peak in performance in the New England sample at around age 40, the age trend in these results appears very similar to that in the Army data. Taken together, therefore, the Army Alpha results from the military officers in World War I and the results from the Jones and Conrad study suggest that there is a fairly pronounced negative relation between age and cognitive performance that apparently cannot be attributed to biased sampling across different segments of the life span.

Although group-administered intelligence tests had proved useful for purposes of classification, a need was perceived for an individually administered intelligence test that could be used to assist in the evaluation of individuals in clinical settings. Wechsler addressed this need in 1939 by publishing the Wechsler-Bellevue Scale designed to assess the intellectual level of adults. The original Wechsler-Bellevue consisted of 10 subtests divided into verbal tests, resembling the Army Alpha, and performance tests, resembling the Army Beta. In 1955, the scale was revised and expanded by adding an 11th subtest measuring vocabulary; it was revised again in 1981.

Norms from the three versions of the Wechsler battery provide valuable information about the relation between age and cognitive performance because in each case the samples were relatively large and fairly representative of the general population. The means at each age of the summed scale scores across the subtests from each edition of the battery are illustrated in Figure 3. As with the Army Alpha data, the results from the Wechsler batteries indicate that increased age is associated with progressively lower performance on measures of cognitive functioning. Wechsler was so convinced that age-related declines of this type were normal that he introduced an age adjustment for the estimation of intellectual level in his scale. This is the reason why, in the Wechsler tests, a 60-year-old can be assigned the same intelligence quotient as a 25-year-old even if he or she performs at a poorer overall level and achieves a lower total score. In fact, the scores displayed in this figure, after being adjusted for age, all correspond to an intelligence quotient of 100 for individuals in the respective age groups.

Intelligence test batteries such as the Army Alpha and the Wechsler scales have been criticized on the grounds that the tests assess an unknown mixture of intellectual abilities, and that the subtests were chosen with little or no theoretical rationale. These objections have led to the development of a number of alternative instruments to assess

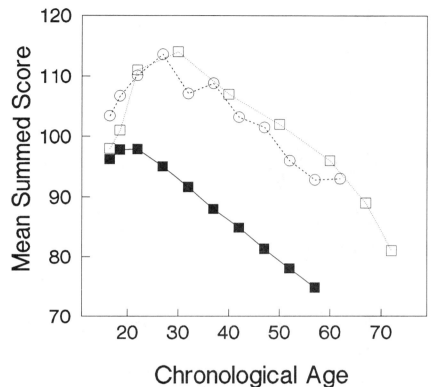

Figure 3. Mean sum of scaled scores at each age from the normative samples of the Wechsler-Bellevue Intelligence Scale (1939)—■, Wechsler Adult Intelligence Scale (1955)—○, and Wechsler Adult Intelligence Scale–Revised (1981)—□. Data and tests cited by permission of Oxford University Press and the Psychological Corporation.

intellectual status. Fortunately, age-comparative data are available for at least several of these alternatives. For example, Thurstone's Primary Mental Abilities Test (L. L. Thurstone & T. G. Thurstone, 1946) was developed on the basis of factor analyses of a large number of cognitive tests to sample what were assumed to be primary mental abilities. Schaie (e.g., 1983) has used a version of this test battery in much of his research, and has reported data on the primary mental abilities of more than 2,800 people who were tested on 4 separate occasions. Results from the composite intellectual ability measure in his project, expressed in t-score units with a mean of 50 and a standard deviation of 10, are illustrated in Figure 4. These results suggest that cognitive performance as assessed by the Primary Mental Ability measures appears to remain relatively

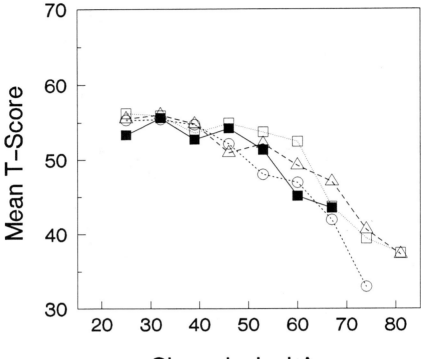

Figure 4. Mean *t* score at each age on the Primary Mental Abilities tests in 1956 (■), 1963 (○), 1970 (□), and 1977 (△). Data are derived from Schaie (1983).

stable until the decade of the 50s, at which point a progressively accelerating decline becomes evident. This is a somewhat different pattern than that found with other measures of cognition, such as those illustrated in the previous figures. One factor that may contribute to the later decline observed in the Primary Mental Ability measures is that the test has a relatively low level of difficulty because it was originally intended for the evaluation of adolescents between 11 and 17 years of age.

One of the few theoretically derived intelligence tests is the Raven's Progressive Matrices, because it was designed to measure what Spearman (1923) considered the essence of *g*, namely, the capacity to apprehend relationships. Problems in the test consist of matrices in which all but one of the cells contain geometric patterns. The patterns within each row and column have a certain relation to one another, and the task for the examinee is to discern those relations in order to select the pattern appropriate for the missing cell.

Heron and Chown (1967) administered the Raven's Progressive Matrices to 540 adults between 20 and 80 years of age under conditions that allowed assessment of scores after 20 minutes, and again after 40 minutes. Results from their study are illustrated in Figure 5. Notice that there is a gradual but systematic decrease in scores with increased age at both the 20-minute and the 40-minute intervals.

Of course, there are many other studies that have compared adults of different ages on standardized cognitive tests; however, I believe that the results just described are generally representative of the literature. It therefore seems reasonable to conclude that the phenomenon of age-related differences in cognitive processes has been reasonably well established. What is not clear from the discussion thus far is whether similar age-related trends are evident in all types of cognition, and what factors are responsible for the declines that have been observed. It is to these topics that I now turn.

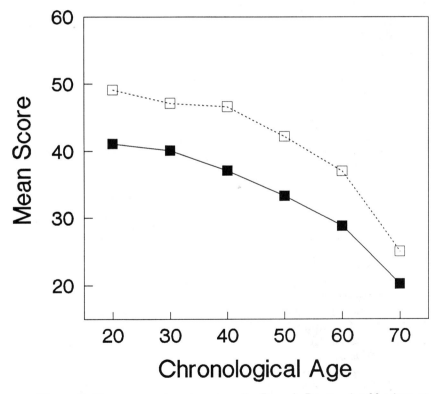

Figure 5. Mean score at each age on the Raven's Progressive Matrices at 20-minute (■) and 40-minute (□) time intervals. Data are derived from Heron and Chown (1967).

Distinctions Among Types of Cognition

Almost since the first age-comparative results on cognition were available, researchers were making distinctions between measures of cognition that exhibited age-related decline and those that did not. For example, in 1928 Thorndike and his colleagues (Thorndike, Bregman, Tilton, & Woodyard, 1928) suggested that "age exerts its most adverse influence upon native capacity or 'sheer modifiability' " (p. 106). And, in 1933, Jones and Conrad claimed that "much of effective intellectual power of the adult [is] derived from accumulated stocks of information" (p. 254). In 1927, Hollingworth was one of the first to combine these two aspects in his statement that "with increasing age . . . learning capacity declines while . . . ability to utilize factors already acquired are still at their maximum" (p. 311).

Two of the most influential classifications of cognitive processes are Hebb's distinction between Type A and Type B intelligence, and Cattell's distinction between fluid and crystallized intelligence. Hebb (1942) argued that intellectual performance was determined by two factors: the capacity to develop new patterns of response, which he referred to as Intelligence A, and the functioning of those patterns already developed, which he termed Intelligence B. He also claimed that the two types of abilities were highly correlated during the period of development, but that they diverged once maturity was reached, with Type A processes declining with age and Type B processes continuing to increase throughout much of adulthood.

Cattell's (1972) fluid–crystallized distinction is very similar to Hebb's Type A–Type B distinction in that fluid ability is defined as a general ability to discriminate and perceive relations, whereas crystallized ability is postulated to consist of habits or knowledge acquired through the past operation of one's fluid abilities. Along with Horn, Cattell has collected considerable data indicating that both fluid and crystallized abilities increase at least through adolescence, but that across the adult years fluid ability decreases and crystallized ability generally remains stable (e.g., Horn & Cattell, 1967).

The different adult age trends for these two types of cognition can be illustrated with normative data from several subtests of the most recent of the Wechsler Adult Intelligence Scales, the WAIS-R (Wechsler, 1981). The Information and Vocabulary subtests from this battery clearly assess previously accumulated knowledge, in the form of historical or cultural information and word meanings, rather than current ability to process or acquire information. On the other hand, the Block Design subtest, which requires the subject to reproduce novel patterns by manipulating blocks, and the Digit Symbol Substitution subtest, which measures the speed and accuracy with which one substitutes symbols for digits, can be viewed as evaluations of processing efficiency at the time of the test, not as reflections of the accomplishments of processing from earlier periods in the individual's life. Relative performance in these tests at different ages is displayed in Figure 6.

Notice that only with the Block Design and Digit Symbol subtests, which are assumed to assess current processing efficiency, is there a systematic decline in performance with increased age. Little or no age-related trend is apparent for the Information and Vocabulary subtests that are postulated to represent Type B, or crystallized, cognitive ability.

A common feature of most of the distinctions among various types of cognition is that increased age is assumed to be associated with declines in raw intellectual power or current ability to process informa-

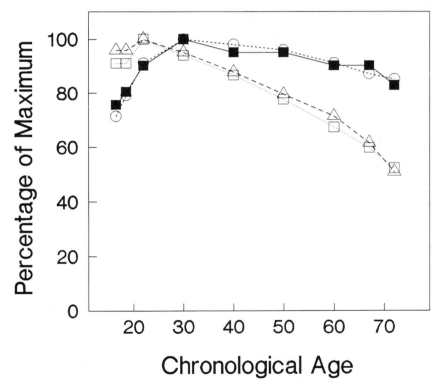

Figure 6. Mean performance at each age as a function of the maximum performance across all ages from the normative samples on four subtests [Information (■), Vocabulary (○), Block Design (□), Digit Symbol (△)] of the Wechsler Adult Intelligence Scale–Revised. Data are derived from Wechsler (1981). Data and test cited by permission of the Psychological Corporation.

tion, but little or no declines are expected in measures of the accumulated products of past cognitive activity. Although the importance of the distinction can be debated, and disputes will probably continue with respect to how it is best expressed, some distinction of this type seems essential in understanding age changes in cognition, because evidence suggests that different measures of cognition vary in their susceptibility to age-related influences.

Considerable evidence seems to support a distinction between process and product types of cognition, but there is still little understanding of the specific mechanisms responsible for the different age-related patterns. For example, stability of the product, Type B, or crystallized measures of cognition is sometimes attributed to an increasing accumulation of cognitive products across one's lifetime. This interpretation has obvious plausibility, but it leads to the expectation that measures of acquired knowledge should increase continuously throughout the adult years. Data of the type summarized in Figure 6 indicate that although performance in tests of previously acquired knowledge does not decrease with age, there are seldom any indications that performance actually increases with age.

Two hypotheses can be proposed to account for the failure to find better performance with increased age in measures of cumulative knowledge. One is that some previously acquired cognitive products may be lost while others are being acquired, such that the net quantity of knowledge remains approximately constant across the adult years. In other words, the total quantity of knowledge may remain stable because old information is lost as rapidly as new information is gained. The second hypothesis is that the information and skills acquired after maturity are progressively more specialized according to one's occupational and avocational interests, whereas items in cognitive test batteries are necessarily rather general in nature in order to be applicable to a broad segment of the population. From this second perspective, therefore, an individual's quantity of knowledge may continue to increase as he or she grows older, but the available tests may no longer be sensitive to the particular types of information that have been acquired. Unfortunately, the relative contributions of these two factors to the age trends in the product, Type B, or crystallized cognitive abilities have apparently not yet been investigated.

A large number of hypotheses have been proposed to account for the age-related declines observed in the process, Type A, or fluid cognitive abilities. Because distinguishing among these alternatives has been a primary goal of researchers for many decades and still represents one of the greatest challenges in the psychology of aging field, several of the most important of the hypotheses are examined in the next section.

Hypotheses on Cognitive Decline

Each of the hypotheses presented here has a moderate amount of support, or at least a considerable degree of intuitive appeal, for otherwise it would not have attained the status of a dominant hypothesis. Unfortunately, a detailed review of both the positive and negative evidence for each hypothesis is beyond the scope of this chapter. Instead, I provide a brief description of each perspective, followed by a discussion of a few of the results that appear to be inconsistent with that view. This strategy of focusing on the weaknesses of each hypothesis and ignoring the strengths runs the risk of conveying an excessively pessimistic impression. It is nevertheless a very efficient means of indicating the limitations of our current state of knowledge about why effectiveness of cognitive functioning changes with increased age.

The Speed Hypothesis

One of the earliest hypotheses proposed to account for the adult age-related differences observed in scores of standardized intelligence tests is that they are attributable to age-related reductions in the speed of peripheral sensory or motor processes. That is, many of the tests included in intelligence batteries are administered with time limits that allow few people to complete all items. It has therefore been suggested that much of the age-related decline in test performance may not be due to actual cognitive impairments; it might instead be caused by a slowing with age in the speed of perceiving or encoding the test items, or in the speed of speaking or writing answers. This view has some credibility because a slowing of perceptual and motor processes with increased age has been established as one of the best-documented phenomena in the entire psychology of aging field (Salthouse, 1985).

It is also true that the items in some timed tests are so easy that they are nearly always answered correctly. Consequently, most of the variation across people occurs in the number of items completed in the allotted time, not in the accuracy of the items that are completed. Removing the time limits from tests such as these would probably result in the elimination of age-related differences in performance, thereby contributing to the belief that the age-related differences originate solely because of slower perceptual–motor processes with increased age.

A number of findings are also clearly inconsistent with a simple speed interpretation. For example, the results of Heron and Chown described earlier, in which similar age trends were evident on the Raven's Progressive Matrices with normal time limits and with double time limits, suggest that sensory–motor speed cannot account for all of the age-related declines in cognitive performance. Further evidence against the view that older adults perform poorly on cognitive tests because of insufficient time to complete all items is available in studies with discrete presentations of the items. As an example, in a recent study of mine, in collaboration with Kausler and Saults (1988), each of 233 adults attempted to solve individually presented geometric analogy problems. Both the median time per problem and the percentage of problems correctly solved served as measures of performance in this task. The means of these values at each decade are displayed in Figure 7. It is clear from these data that not only did the time required to reach a solution increase with age, but that there was also a decrease in the average accuracy of those solutions.

Results of the type just discussed seem to rule out the hypothesis that most of the age-related declines in cognitive performance are simply attributable to slower perceptual–motor processes. It is probably true that slower writing speed contributes to the age declines in some tests, and slowing of peripheral processes may be responsible for a substantial

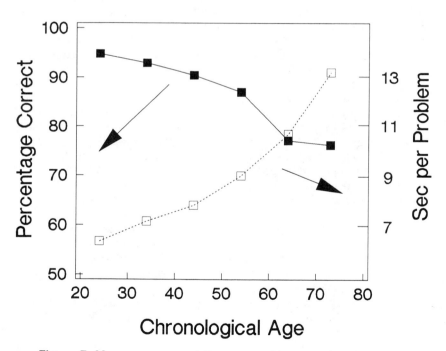

Figure 7. Mean accuracy and time per problem as a function of age for geometric analogy problems. Data are derived from Salthouse, Kausler, and Saults (1988).

portion of the age differences observed in very easy tests. The existence of sizable age-related declines in power tests with generous time limits and of declines in the accuracy of individually timed items suggests, however, that slower perceptual–motor processes do not explain the phenomenon entirely.

It is important in discussing the speed interpretation that a distinction be drawn between peripheral slowing and central slowing. As was just mentioned, the available evidence is not consistent with the view that a slowing of peripheral perceptual–motor processes is responsible for most of the age-related declines in cognitive functioning. It is still possible, however, that an age-related slowing of central or cognitive processes contributes in some way to the observed cognitive differences. Unfortunately, it has been difficult to evaluate this hypothesis because of the problems of measuring the speed of central processes and of relating the quickness of cognitive operations to the quality of the products of those operations. Nevertheless, the central-slowing version of the speed hypothesis still appears viable and should be differentiated from the peripheral-slowing version, which has been found to be inadequate to account for much of the age-related declines observed in cognitive performance.

The Disuse Hypothesis

A second very influential hypothesis proposed to account for findings that performance on certain types of intellectual or cognitive tests is lower at increased ages is loosely known as the disuse hypothesis. There are several different versions of this hypothesis, and each has at least some plausibility. For example, it is frequently observed that many contemporary intelligence tests were originally designed for the assessment of children in school situations, and that increased age is generally associated with a greater elapsed time from the period of school attendance. It has therefore been argued that if cognitive abilities decline with disuse, at least some cognitive declines may be attributable to lack of recent exercise of those abilities.

Although the disuse perspective is still quite popular, a variety of empirical results seem to suggest that it can account for very little of the age-related declines observed in measures of cognitive functioning. However, because this perspective has been, and continues to be, extremely influential, it is important to carefully consider the type of evidence that appears to contradict the disuse interpretation of age-related cognitive differences.

One expectation from the disuse perspective is that age-related declines should be minimal to nonexistent for activities continuously performed throughout one's lifetime, because no disuse has occurred that could have caused the decline. Very little detailed information is available concerning the actual frequency of various types of activities at different ages, but sizable age-related differences have been reported for a number of tasks that seem to resemble fairly common activities. For example, many researchers have reported that increased age is associated with poorer performance in tests of memory for information presented in stories and in other meaningful discourse. Figure 8 displays the results from one study (Randt, Brown, & Osborne, 1980) in which recall of a short story was tested immediately after presentation of the story, and again after 24 hours. Although people frequently try to describe the details of recently experienced events or to repeat stories or instructions they have heard, the results of this study, and those of many others, suggest that the ability to recall meaningful material decreases systematically with increased age.

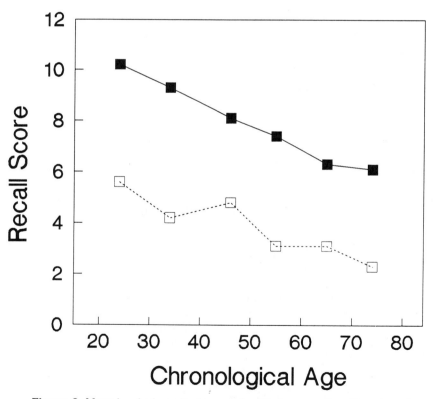

Figure 8. Mean level of recall of a meaningful story as a function of age for immediate (■) and for 24-hour (□) tests. Data are derived from Randt, Brown, and Osborne (1980).

Randt et al. also evaluated the accuracy with which participants in their project could identify the activities they had performed while participating in the project. Recall of recently performed activities can be argued to be very similar to what occurs in many real-life situations, as is evidenced by the frequency of queries such as "Did you remember to lock the door?" or "Are you sure you turned off the stove?" Their results, summarized in Figure 9, indicate, however, that even this type of memory, which is presumably high in ecological validity, has been found to decrease systematically with increased age.

There have also been a number of reports of age-related differences in people tested for memory and reasoning ability when the problems were presented in familiar, and presumably frequently experienced, contexts. For example, young adults have been found to perform better than older adults in remembering familiar sayings (e.g., Wood & Pratt, 1987), in remembering the source of acquired information (e.g., McIntyre & Craik, 1987), and in remembering to perform an intended action (e.g.,

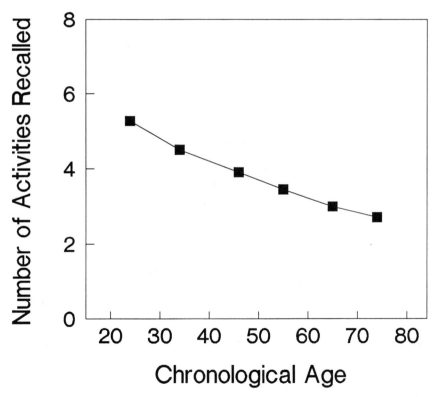

Figure 9. Mean number of previously performed activities correctly recalled as a function of age. Data are derived from Randt, Brown, and Osborne (1980).

Dobbs & Rule, 1987). Age-related differences favoring young adults have also been reported in people tested for reasoning ability with problems presented in everyday language (e.g., Cohen, 1981), for the ability to make inferences and deductions based on information presented in newspaper stories (e.g., Friend & Zubek, 1958), and for the ability to adjust recipes to different proportions (e.g., Hooper, Hooper, & Colbert, 1984).

Comparisons have also been made of the age trends among people who performed concrete and abstract versions of the same task. These comparisons are relevant to the disuse hypothesis because it has been suggested that after formal schooling is completed, most natural problem solving deals with concrete situations, rather than with abstract problems of the type contained in intelligence tests and experimental cognitive tasks. Another implication from the disuse perspective, therefore, is that age differences should be less pronounced in people performing concrete tasks involving familiar materials than in those performing abstract tasks containing arbitrary or unfamiliar materials.

One study relevant to the abstract–concrete issue was reported by Hayslip and Sterns (1979). These researchers administered two versions of a concept identification task to three groups of adults. The abstract version of the task was a typical concept identification task in which the stimuli varied in attributes such as shape, color, and size, and the feedback consisted of reports that the stimulus was either positive or negative. The concrete version of the task was a "poisoned foods" task introduced by Arenberg (1968), in which the stimuli were meals consisting of meat, a vegetable, and a beverage, and the feedback consisted of information about whether the diner lived or died. Figure 10 illustrates that the format in which the problems were presented had relatively little effect on the age relationships, because very similar patterns were evident in the abstract and concrete versions of the task.

Another expectation of the disuse hypothesis is that people who are in mentally demanding occupations should not experience the age-related cognitive declines typical of other samples of adults. The rationale for this prediction is that most cognitive processes can be assumed to be in more or less continuous use for people in intellectually stimulating occupations, and thus no declines attributable to disuse should occur. One of the best studies investigating this expectation was reported by Sward in 1945. The participants in his research project were all faculty members at two prestigious universities, and special efforts were taken to ensure that young (21 to 45 years old) and old (60 to 79 years old) faculty participants were matched with respect to academic field of specialization, frequency of membership in honorary societies, and so forth. Results from the eight tests in his study, only two of which were administered under speeded conditions, are displayed in Figure 11. This figure shows the percentage of older adults whose scores exceeded the median scores of the young adults; hence all the bars would be at the 50-percent value if the two groups did not differ in any of the measures.

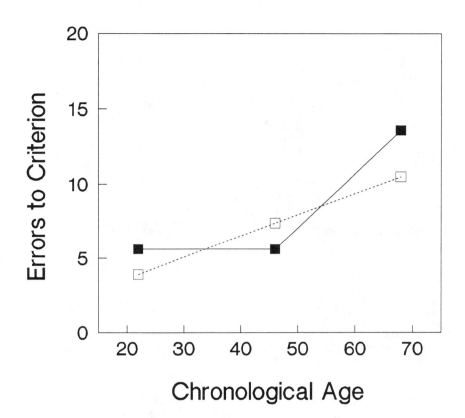

Figure 10. Mean number of errors to criterion in abstract (■) and concrete (□) concept identification tasks as a function of age. Data are derived from Hayslip and Sterns (1979).

It can be seen, however, that with the exception of one of the tests of previously acquired information (i.e., the synonym–antonym test), faculty members ranging from 21 to 42 years of age performed much better than did most of their colleagues whose ages were between 60 and 79.

One of the most controversial aspects of the disuse hypothesis deals with the anticipated effects of training on subjects of different ages in measures of cognitive functioning. Much of the controversy concerns the question of whether adults of different ages need to be compared with respect to the magnitude of training-related benefits. From the perspective of some researchers, a discovery that older adults can improve their performance on cognitive tests with relatively modest amounts of training is sufficient to establish that there is considerable plasticity in their cognitive functioning, and consequently that age-related declines are potentially reversible. Other researchers, however, have argued that it is

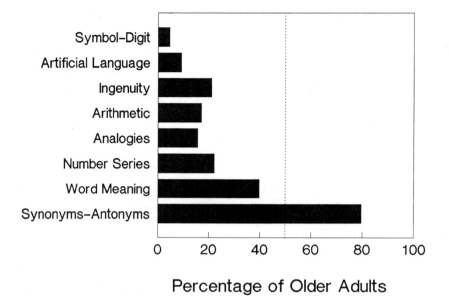

Percentage of Older Adults

Figure 11. Percentage of older adults whose scores exceeded the median scores of younger adults across eight cognitive tests. Data are derived from Sward (1945).

quite conceivable that young adults would exhibit comparable training-related cognitive improvement, in which case no age-specific interpretation would be warranted. Only by administering the same training regimen to adults of different ages, these researchers argue, is it possible to separate age-independent effects of training from the effects attributable to the remediation of disuse.

Despite the controversy regarding the appropriate design of developmentally relevant training studies, the available results from both age-homogeneous and age-comparative training studies have been remarkably consistent. The dominant finding from studies with only older adult participants is that performance of older adults on a variety of cognitive tests can be improved with several different types of training (e.g., see Willis, 1987, for a review). Although the theoretical significance of this finding for the interpretation of cognitive phenomena among the aging continues to be hotly debated, it is potentially of considerable practical importance. That is, because the results of these studies have demonstrated that certain training procedures are effective in increasing the cognitive performance of older adults, there is reason to be optimistic about the success of many educational and training programs designed for older workers.

As an aside, it is interesting to note that studies of training with older adults can be considered to occupy a unique status within psychology because they represent one of the few areas of research in which William James has been proven to be completely wrong. That is, in nearly every area of contemporary psychology, James is revered for having anticipated results that have only recently received empirical confirmation. The results that successful training can occur in older adults, however, clearly refute James's assertion that "outside of their own business, the ideas gained by men before they are twenty-five are practically the only ideas they shall have in their lives. They cannot get anything new" (1890, p. 402).

There have been only a handful of age-comparative training studies, but most have been consistent in demonstrating that young adults improve at least as much with training or practice as do older adults. The results of one study (Kamin, 1957), comparing the effects of four sessions of practice on the performance of young (high school students of unspecified age) and older (age 65 to 85) adults on the Primary Mental Abilities Test, are displayed in Figure 12. The performance axis in this figure is the percentile from the test norms corresponding to the mean performance of each group in each session. Notice that, if anything, the young adults in this study had greater gains across successive sessions than did the older adults. Findings of this type are clearly inconsistent with the disuse perspective, because the training gains of young adults match or exceed those of older adults, yet it is not plausible to argue that the young adults are also suffering from a disuse-mediated cognitive deficit. The implication seems to be that the benefits of training must be attributed to factors other than the remediation of disuse, because they have also been found to occur in samples of young adults for whom little or no disuse could have occurred.

Let me briefly summarize the research I have reviewed relevant to the disuse hypothesis of age-related cognitive decline. First, it was noted that age-related differences favoring young adults are frequently found in activities similar to those performed in everyday life, and with both concrete and abstract versions of reasoning tasks. Second, it was reported that age-related differences in measures of cognitive functioning have been found in samples composed entirely of university professors, a population for whom mental processes might be expected to be in continuous use. And finally, results from studies of the effects of training were summarized indicating that both older and young adults benefit from training. No single category of research is by itself definitive with respect to the disuse hypothesis; however, the failure to confirm expectations across several different types of comparisons raises serious questions about the validity of the view that lack of exercise of cognitive processes is responsible for the age-related differences observed in measures of cognitive functioning.

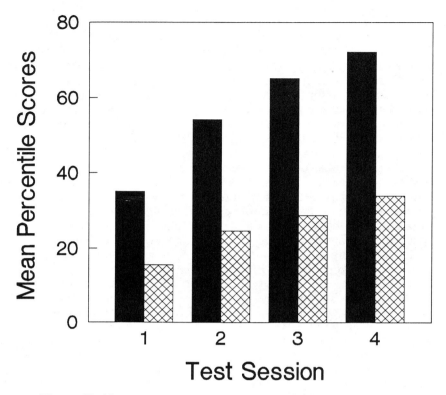

Figure 12. Mean percentile scores of young (solid bars) and older adults (cross-hatched bars) on the Primary Mental Abilities Test as a function of four sessions of practice. Data are derived from Kamin (1957).

The Changing-Environment Hypothesis

The third major hypothesis proposed to account for age-related cognitive declines is that the individual does not change, but aspects of the physical or social environment are constantly changing such that successive generations of people perform progressively better on the same tests. For example, the height of the average adult has increased over the last century, apparently because of improvements in nutrition and public health practices, and it is conceivable that changes in the social or cultural environment may have contributed to higher levels of performance on many cognitive tests. From the perspective of this hypothesis, therefore, the important question is not what causes the age-related declines, but rather, what changing aspects of the environment are responsible for the improved levels of test performance achieved by more recent generations of test takers?

One category of evidence relevant to the changing-environment hypothesis consists of the results of time-lag analyses in which comparisons are made of the performance of people of the same age taking the same test at different times. If the environment is changing in a manner that results in higher levels of cognitive functioning among the people entering the environment most recently, then one should expect higher test scores by people of the same age taking the same test at later, or more recent, times. Evidence for this prediction appears to be somewhat mixed. On the one hand, results such as those illustrated earlier to indicate the age trends in the Primary Mental Abilities test results suggest that there has been relatively little systematic effect of environmental change on cognitive functioning. That is, very similar mean levels, and patterns across age, were apparent in the Schaie data displayed in Figure 4 from people who were administered the Primary Mental Abilities Test in 1956, 1963, 1970, and 1977. On the other hand, several large-scale analyses (e.g., Flynn, 1987; Parker, 1986) have revealed that mean performance on some intellectual tests does appear to have increased across successive generations. One particularly impressive finding of this type is the report by Tuddenham (1948) that a sample of 768 U.S. Army soldiers, who were administered the Army Alpha during World War II, had an average score at the 83rd percentile of the norms from tests administered during World War I.

Some researchers have suggested that many of the time-lag effects, and thus, indirectly, the age-related cognitive differences, are attributable to improvements over time in educational opportunity. This has been a difficult argument to evaluate. On the one hand, it is quite true that the average number of years of education has increased across successive generations. On the other hand, there is considerable debate over whether the actual quality of education has improved, and it can even be questioned whether the number of years of school attendance is a causal determinant of performance in tests of intelligence.

Reports that age-related differences are minimized when research participants are equated with respect to years of education (e.g., Birren & Morrison, 1961; Green, 1969) are sometimes interpreted as support for the importance of education to age-related differences in cognition. Unfortunately, studies of this type are often ambiguous because of the dramatic changes that have taken place with regard to the accessibility of a college education. That is, 40 years ago college attendance was more closely associated than at present with factors known to be correlated with performance on intelligence tests, such as parents' income, occupations, and general socioeconomic status. In this respect, therefore, equating young and older adults according to the amount of formal education they have received may have the effect of biasing intellectual ability in favor of the older adults, in which case the age trends in measures of cognitive functioning would probably be spurious.

One version of the changing-environment hypothesis postulates that much of what are assumed to be age-related differences are actually cohort differences. Cohort in this context refers to people born within a given temporal interval, who thus experience the same environmental and sociocultural events at similar periods in their lives. Certain aspects of the nature and timing of physical and cultural events are presumably critical for the occurrence of the hypothesized cohort effects, but a weakness of this perspective is that these critical aspects have not yet been identified by researchers working within this framework. The inability to identify the relevant variables has obviously made it difficult to subject the cohort hypothesis to rigorous analytical investigation.

One of the strongest proponents of the cohort interpretation has been Schaie, who has also been responsible for collecting the largest amount of data relevant to the evaluation of this perspective. I present Schaie's results in the context of an important prediction of the cohort perspective. It should be mentioned that the present analyses, based on the most complete report of the published data available from Schaie's Seattle Longitudinal study (1983), lead to somewhat different conclusions than those previously reached by Schaie and his colleagues on the basis of earlier analyses of portions of these data. The reasons for these differences are not completely clear, but it is important to emphasize that the present inferences are based on the largest samples available from Schaie's own data.

The simplest and strongest implication of the cohort perspective is that no age-related differences should be evident when the age comparisons are carried out within the same cohort. That is, if the age-related differences typically observed in cross-sectional studies are due to factors associated with cohort membership rather than to chronological age, then those differences should disappear if the contrasts involve people of different ages but from the same cohort. There are two methods by which the confounding of age and cohort inherent in cross-sectional studies can be avoided. Both involve extending the period for the collection of data across several years, so that people from the same cohort can be tested at different ages. As an example, people born in 1930 might be tested in 1960 when they were 30 years old, in 1970 when they were 40 years old, and again in 1980 when they were 50 years old. The two methods differ with respect to whether the same or different individuals are tested at each occasion. When the same people are tested at each occasion, the contrasts provide the classical longitudinal design. For the sake of simplicity, I refer to the version involving independent groups of people at each measurement occasion as the same-cohort design.

The prediction in both the longitudinal and same-cohort comparisons is that if cross-sectional age-related differences are actually reflections of variations across cohorts, then there should be little or no effects of age when the age comparisons are carried out within the same cohort. Results relevant to these predictions are displayed in Figure 13. This figure shows estimates of the mean composite intellectual ability difference in *t*-score units across a 7-year interval. The different curves represent the traditional cross-sectional comparison; the longitudinal comparison; and the independent groups, same-cohort comparison. The important point to note from these results is that the three functions are all very similar to one another. This analysis of Schaie's data therefore implies that cohort factors do not appear to be responsible for many of the age-related differences observed in cross-sectional studies, because equivalent age-related differences are also evident in comparisons within the same-birth cohort.

Perhaps the best method of investigating the hypothesis that age-related behavioral differences are caused by changes in the external

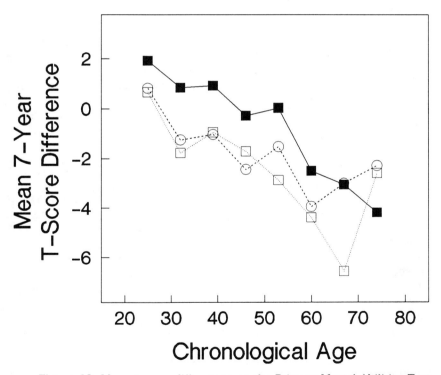

Figure 13. Mean *t*-score differences on the Primary Mental Abilities Test across a seven-year interval for cross-sectional (different people, different cohorts—□), longitudinal (same people, same cohort—■), and same cohort (different people, same cohort—○) samples. Data are derived from Schaie (1983).

environment rather than by internal changes in the organism is to determine whether there are still systematic effects of age when one is confident that the environment has not changed. In most comparisons of human behavior it is difficult, if not impossible, to be confident that the environment has remained invariant, because of the complexity of human environments and the relatively long human life spans. One can have much more confidence that the environment has remained constant, however, if the relevant behavior can be observed in lower animals, because rigorous control can be exerted over almost all aspects of their environment from birth to death.

Research on age-related effects in animals should therefore prove very informative about the changing-environment hypothesis. That is, if this hypothesis is correct, few or no age-related differences should be observed in animals living in stable and controlled environments. There are obviously some limitations in the generalizations that can be drawn about human behavior from research with animals, but the inferential leaps can be minimized if one examines similar types of behavior across different species.

One behavioral measure that has been examined in humans and in animals raised in relatively controlled environments is the accuracy of reproducing target cells in a spatial matrix. A version of this task administered to human research participants consisted of a 3-s presentation of a 5 × 5 matrix, with 7 of the 25 cells highlighted as targets. Shortly after the stimulus matrix was removed, a blank matrix was displayed and the individual was asked to designate which cells had been targets in the previous display. The mean number of cells correctly reproduced at each decade for 362 adults in a recent study of mine, in collaboration with Kausler and Saults (1988), is illustrated in Figure 14.

Figure 15 shows the results from two studies involving a similar task with rhesus monkeys (Bartus, Fleming, & Johnson, 1978; Medin, 1969). Both studies consisted of a brief presentation of a lighted cell in a matrix, and after a short, dark interval, the monkey was allowed to reach and touch the previously illuminated panel to receive a reward. The studies differed in several respects, including the ages of the two groups of monkeys, the retention interval between the initial presentation and the subsequent test (either 10 s or 15 s for the conditions illustrated in Figures 14 and 15), and in the complexity of the stimulus matrix (either 3 × 3 or 4 × 4). It can be seen, however, that despite these procedural differences, the results of the two studies were nearly identical.

Figure 14 and Figure 15 indicate that very similar trends for increased age to be associated with lower spatial memory performance are evident in the human data and in the data of rhesus monkeys. This parallelism, together with reports of age-related differences in a variety of species with tasks ranging from one-trial passive avoidance (e.g., Bartus, Dean, Goas, & Lippa, 1980), to complex maze learning (e.g., Goodrick, 1972),

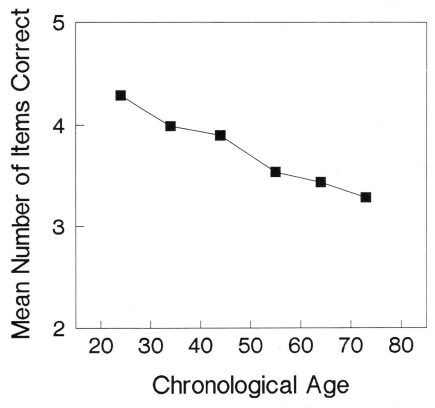

Figure 14. Mean number of spatial matrix target cells correctly recalled as a function of age for humans. Data are derived from Salthouse, Kausler, and Saults (1988).

strongly suggests that age-related declines in cognitive processes occur even in the absence of changes in the external environment.

The available evidence therefore does not appear very consistent with the hypothesis that a substantial proportion of the age-related differences observed in measures of cognitive functioning are attributable to changes in the external environment rather than to changes taking place within the organism. It is difficult to explain the documented cases of positive time-lag effects, in which successive generations have been found to score progressively higher on the same test, without reference to changes in the physical or cultural environment. The factors that might be responsible for these changes have thus far proven elusive. Educational practices and the quantity of formal education are frequently mentioned possibilities, but it has been difficult to document these

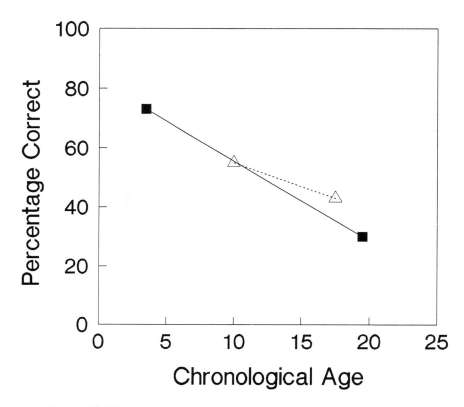

Figure 15. Mean percentage of correct responses in a delayed-response spatial matrix task as a function of age for rhesus monkeys. Data are derived from Bartus, Fleming, and Johnson (1978), and Medin (1969).

influences. Considerable attention has been focused on the idea that age-related differences might actually be attributable to cohort differences, but analyses based on the most complete data available suggest that the age differences within the same cohorts are nearly as large as those found across different cohorts. Finally, the existence of substantial age-related differences in the behavior of animals raised under constant and rigorously controlled environmental conditions implies that many of the effects related to age are due to biologically based changes originating inside the organism.

Current Hypotheses

The preceding survey of major hypotheses suggests that there is a moderate amount of contradictory evidence for each of the historically prominent hypotheses of age-related decline. Although it is still too early to reject these views completely, many contemporary researchers have pursued a number of alternative perspectives in seeking explanations for age-related cognitive decline. A detailed review of all of the current efforts is not possible in this chapter, but I will describe two in order to indicate the type of research currently being conducted to address the question of what is responsible for age-related cognitive decline.

One very active category of research can be termed componential analysis, because the focus has been on analyzing cognitive activities in terms of their hypothesized elementary components. For example, many contemporary researchers have adopted an information-processing perspective and have tried to specify what aspects of the information processing required in a given cognitive task present the most problems to older adults. A major issue to be resolved within the componential analysis perspective concerns the appropriate, or optimal, level of analysis and description. Much of the research thus far has consisted of attempts to provide fairly precise descriptions of the processing within a particular cognitive task, but such descriptions often have limited generality to other tasks. The challenge facing researchers employing this approach, therefore, will be to identify a level of analysis that is meaningful for specific tasks and yet is at a high enough level of abstraction to be applicable to a variety of different tasks, and to provide a potential basis for ultimate explanation at the anatomical or physiological level.

A second area of current research concerns the influence of health status on age-related cognitive decline. The idea that health or disease factors contribute to lower cognitive performance with increased age is plausible, because a variety of diseases have been found to depress the level of cognitive functioning, and the incidence of many diseases tends to increase with age. One of the obstacles impeding progress in this area seems to be the lack of a quick and inexpensive, but valid, index of an individual's health status. The three techniques currently available—self-assessed health on one or more dimensions, an objective checklist, and examination by a physician—all have weaknesses that limit their usefulness in certain situations. The degree of correspondence among the measures is also largely unknown because few large-scale studies have been reported in which all three types of evaluations were obtained.

Conclusion

I have discussed three aspects of cognitive changes that occur with age, which might be characterized as the when, what, and why of the phenomenon of age-related cognitive decline. These aspects are all interrelated, and consequently it is necessary to identify what type of cognition is of interest before attempting to address the question of when or why any age-related changes occur. Sufficient data are available to determine that the age-related differences are often detectable in relatively large samples of young adults, although the onset of the phenomenon varies greatly across different cognitive measures. Causes for the phenomenon have been actively investigated, but the best conclusion at the present time is that none of the simple explanations seems adequate to account for the age-related cognitive decline phenomenon.

References

Arenberg, D. (1968). Concept problem solving in young and old adults. *Journal of Gerontology, 23*, 279–282.

Bartus, R. T., Dean, R. L., Goas, J. A., & Lippa, A. S. (1980). Age-related changes in passive avoidance retention: Modulation with dietary choline. *Science, 209*, 301–303.

Bartus, R. T., Fleming, D., & Johnson, H. R. (1978). Aging in the rhesus monkey: Debilitating effects on short-term memory. *Journal of Gerontology, 33*, 858–871.

Birren, J. E., & Morrison, D. F. (1961). Analysis of the WAIS subtests in relation to age and education. *Journal of Gerontology, 16*, 363–369.

Cattell, R. B. (1972). *Abilities: Their structure, growth, and action.* Boston: Houghton Mifflin.

Cohen, G. (1981). Inferential reasoning in old age. *Cognition, 9*, 59–72.

Dobbs, A. R., & Rule, B. G. (1987). Prospective memory and self-reports of memory abilities in older adults. *Canadian Journal of Psychology, 41*, 209–222.

Flynn, J. R. (1987). Massive IQ gains in 14 nations: What IQ tests really measure. *Psychological Bulletin, 101*, 171–191.

Friend, C. M., & Zubek, J. P. (1958). The effects of age on critical thinking ability. *Journal of Gerontology, 13*, 407–413.

Goodrick, C. L. (1972). Learning by mature-young and aged Wistar albino rats as a function of test complexity. *Journal of Gerontology, 27*, 353–357.

Green, R. F. (1969). Age–intelligence relationship between ages sixteen and sixty-four: A rising trend. *Developmental Psychology, 1*, 618–627.

Hayslip, B., & Sterns, H. L. (1979). Age differences in relationships between crystallized and fluid intelligences and problem solving. *Journal of Gerontology, 34*, 404–414.

Hebb, D. O. (1942). The effect of early and late brain injury upon test scores, and the nature of normal adult intelligence. *Proceedings of the American Philosophical Society, 85*, 275–292.

Heron, A., & Chown, S. M. (1967). *Age and function.* Boston: Little, Brown.

Hollingworth, H. L. (1927). *Mental growth and decline.* New York: Appleton.

Hooper, F. H., Hooper, J. O., & Colbert, K. C. (1984). *Personality and memory correlates of intellectual functioning: Young adulthood to old age.* Basel, Switzerland: Karger.

Horn, J. L., & Cattell, R. B. (1967). Age differences in fluid and crystallized intelligence. *Acta Psychologica, 26*, 107–129.

James, W. (1890). *Principles of psychology* (Vol. 2). New York: Holt.

Jones, H. E., & Conrad, H. S. (1933). The growth and decline of intelligence: A study of a homogeneous group between the ages of ten and sixty. *Genetic Psychological Monographs, 13*, 223–298.

Kamin, L. J. (1957). Differential changes in mental abilities in old age. *Journal of Gerontology, 12*, 66–70.

Koga, Y., & Morant, G. M. (1923). On the degree of association between reaction times in the case of different senses. *Biometrika, 15*, 346–372.

Labouvie-Vief, G., & Chandler, M. J. (1978). Cognitive development and life-span developmental theory: Idealistic versus contextualistic perspectives. In P. B. Baltes (Ed.), *Life-span development and behavior* (Vol. 1, pp. 181–210). New York: Academic Press.

McIntyre, J. S., & Craik, F. I. M. (1987). Age differences in memory for item and source information. *Canadian Journal of Psychology, 41*, 175–192.

Medin, D. L. (1969). Form perception and pattern reproduction by monkeys. *Journal of Comparative and Physiological Psychology, 68*, 412–419.

Parker, K. C. (1986). Changes with age, year-of-birth cohort, age by year-of-birth cohort interaction and standardization of the Wechsler Adult Intelligence Tests. *Human Development, 29*, 209–222.

Randt, C. T., Brown, E. R., & Osborne, D. P. (1980). A memory test for longitudinal measurement of mild to moderate deficits. *Clinical Neuropsychology, 2*, 184–194.

Salthouse, T. A. (1985). Speed of behavior and its implications for cognition. In J. E. Birren & K. W. Schaie (Eds.), *Handbook of the psychology of aging* (2nd ed., pp. 400–426). New York: Van Nostrand Reinhold.

Salthouse, T. A., Kausler, D. H., & Saults, J. S. (1988). Investigation of student status, background variables, and the feasibility of standard tasks in cognitive aging research. *Psychology and Aging, 3*, 29–37.

Schaie, K. W. (1979). The primary mental abilities in adulthood: An exploration in the development of psychometric intelligence. In P. B. Baltes & O. G. Brim (Eds.), *Life-span development and behavior* (Vol. 2, pp. 67–115). New York: Academic Press.

Schaie, K. W. (1983). The Seattle Longitudinal Study: A 21–year exploration of psychometric intelligence in adulthood. In K. W. Schaie (Ed.), *Longitudinal studies of adult psychological development*. New York: Guilford Press.

Spearman, C. (1923). *The nature of intelligence and the principles of cognition*. New York: Macmillan.

Sward, K. (1945). Age and mental ability in superior men. *American Journal of Psychology, 58*, 443–479.

Thorndike, E. L., Bregman, E. O., Tilton, J. W., & Woodyard, E. (1928). *Adult learning*. New York: MacMillan.

Thurstone, L. L. & Thurstone, T. G. (1946). *SRA Primary Mental Abilities*. Chicago: Science Research Associates.

Tuddenham, R. D. (1948). Soldier intelligence in World Wars I and II. *American Psychologist, 3*, 54–56.

Wechsler, D. (1939). *Measurement of adult intelligence*. Baltimore: Williams & Wilkins.

Wechsler, D. (1955). *Manual for the Wechsler Adult Intelligence Scale*. New York: The Psychological Corporation.

Wechsler, D. (1981). *Manual for the Wechsler Adult Intelligence Scale–Revised.* New York: The Psychological Corporation.

Welford, A. T. (1966). Industrial work suitable for older people: Some British studies. *Gerontologist, 6*, 4–9.

Willis, S. L. (1987). Cognitive training and everyday competence. In K.W. Schaie (Ed.), *Annual review of gerontology and geriatrics* (Vol. 7, pp. 159–188). New York: Springer.

Wood, L. E., & Pratt, J. D. (1987). Pegword mnemonic as an aid to memory in the elderly: A comparison of four age groups. *Educational Gerontology, 13*, 325–339.

Yerkes, R. M. (1921). Psychological examining in the United States Army. *Memoirs of the National Academy of Sciences, 15*, 1–877.

PERSONALITY CONTINUITY AND THE CHANGES OF ADULT LIFE

Paul T. Costa, Jr., is the Chief of the Laboratory of Personality and Cognition in the National Institute on Aging's Gerontology Research Center. He has academic appointments in the Departments of Psychiatry and Behavioral Science of the Johns Hopkins School of Medicine and Duke University School of Medicine and is an adjunct professor in the Department of Psychology, University of Maryland, Baltimore County. Costa is internationally known for his research in the areas of the structure and stability of personality, personality assessment, psychological risk factors for cardiovascular disease, biological and functional aging, and the influence of personality on perceived health and psychological well-being.

In 1970 Costa earned a PhD in human development and clinical psychology from the University of Chicago. He has held faculty appointments at Harvard University and the University of Massachusetts at Boston. Since 1982, he has been editor for the Biobehavioral and Social Sciences Section, *Experimental Aging Research*, and he is on the editorial boards of *Psychology and Aging*, *Health Psychology*, *International Journal of Aging and Human Development*, and the *Journal of Aging and Health*. He has authored or co-authored several books and a standardized personality inventory and has published more than 125 articles.

Costa has been elected a Fellow of the American Psychological Association (APA), the Society of Behavioral Medicine, and the Gerontological Society of America. He has reviewed for the National Science Foundation, the Veterans Administration, and the National Institutes of Health and has chaired and served on several national task forces and advisory committees. He is a past president of the Division of Adult Development and Aging of APA.

PERSONALITY CONTINUITY AND THE CHANGES OF ADULT LIFE

B y dictionary definition, *adult* means "fully developed and mature" (Morris, 1976, p. 18). *Adult development* might therefore be considered an oxymoron, a clever contradiction intended to make us pause and think about when development ends and adulthood begins. But long use in academic circles has robbed the phrase of this effect, and instead we tend to think of adult development as a kind of postgraduate extension of child development. One purpose of this chapter is to raise the question of whether personality development continues past age 18 or 21 or 30, and if not, what other, nondevelopmental models of personality in adulthood might be useful in understanding men and women as they age. Given the current state of knowledge, how should we approach the creation of a psychology of adult life?

Approaches to Studying Adult Development

The Birth of a Field

In the past decade, the "midlife crisis" has become part of mass culture. Although there is virtually no evidence that such a phenomenon occurs (Costa & McCrae, 1980b; Farrell & Rosenberg, 1981), its acceptance in the popular press is evidence of a significant change in thinking about adulthood. Western culture in general has traditionally conceived of adulthood as a plateau extending from adolescence to senescence with neither growth nor crisis, and most psychologists implicitly shared this view until relatively recently. Educational psychologists noted early in the century that the concept of mental age, which made considerable sense when dealing with children, became meaningless after age 18, when intellectual maturity was reached. William James claimed that character was "set like plaster" by age 30, and Freud had very little to say about psychological change after early childhood.

It was therefore a feat of great intellectual daring to propose that psychological development might continue throughout life, and one of history's boldest thinkers, C. G. Jung, was among the earliest and most influential to take this step. His chapter, "The Stages of Life," in *Modern Man in Search of a Soul* (Jung, 1933) foreshadowed many of the central ideas in gerontological thinking, including the curve of life (Bühler, 1935), the rise of the repressed (Levinson, Darrow, Klein, Levinson, & McKee, 1978), the feminization of men and masculinization of women (Gutmann, 1970), disengagement theory (Cumming & Henry, 1961), and the midlife crisis itself.

A more elaborated and systematic position was offered by Erikson (1950), who postulated stages of psychosocial development to parallel Freud's stages of psychosexual development, and then extended them beyond adolescence and across the remaining years of life. Erikson's theory was an integration of biological, cultural, and psychological influences; in the ideal case, the growth of the individual at each stage of life meshed with the needs of other generations. Psychosocial development in adulthood was hypothesized to progress from concerns for *identity* and *intimacy*, needed for entering adult life, to *generativity*, when productivity and childrearing are the central tasks, and finally to *ego integrity*, when life is near completion. Erikson's epigenetic chart is still probably what most introductory psychology students learn about the theory of adult development.

The next few decades saw the beginnings of empirical research on personality and aging, some of it guided by the theories of Erikson (e.g., Constantinople, 1969) or Jung, much of it in search of new theoretical perspectives (Block with Haan, 1971; Butler, 1963; Lowenthal, Thurner, & Chiriboga, 1975; Maas & Kuypers, 1974; Neugarten, 1964; Reichard, Livson, & Peterson, 1962; Shanan, 1985). In the late 1970s, a new generation of theories of adult development appeared (Gould, 1978; Levinson et al., 1978; Vaillant, 1977), Sheehy's (1976) *Passages* became a major bestseller,

---

Paul Costa presented a Master Lecture at the 1988 APA Convention. The lecture was based on this chapter, which was produced in collaboration with Robert R. McCrae, research psychologist at the Personality, Stress, and Coping Section of the National Institute on Aging's Gerontology Research Center.

---

and the popular press began to feature stories on crises in adulthood, particularly the midlife crisis.

During the 1970s, there was also a proliferation of undergraduate and graduate programs in human development and gerontology. Most of these programs were explicitly interdisciplinary, examining the sociology, biology, and economy of aging as well as the psychology. Stage theories of adult development had a powerful appeal as a way of integrating such diverse material: Predictable changes in personality might prepare the individual for the transitions and changes of adult life.

All of these intellectual developments were consistent with the zeitgeist. The 1950s had focused on children, the 1960s on youth. As the baby boomers passed 30, their lives still seemed to form the center of the culture's interest. Personal growth and development were promised by humanistic psychology, and theories of life stages seemed to fill a particular need. Personal problems could be attributed to universal developmental changes; predictable crises offered both security and spice to adult life.

The same period also saw the "graying of America," a dramatic increase in the proportion of men and women living beyond 65, and a concomitant increase in their awareness of their economic and political power. Older people began to demand attention, and academics took up the challenge. Personality development offered an attractive alternative to studies of cognition, where decline, if not inevitable, was the general rule (Arenberg & Robertson-Tchabo, 1977. See also the chapter "Age-Related Changes in Basic Cognitive Processes," by T. A. Salthouse in this volume.).

By happy coincidence, the 1970s also saw the fruits of a series of longitudinal studies of adults initiated years earlier by a number of extraordinarily foresighted scientists who saw the need for beginning studies that others would ultimately finish (Bell, Rose, & Damon, 1972; Eichorn, Clausen, Haan, Honzik, & Mussen, 1981; Kelly, 1955; Palmore, 1970, 1974; Shock et al., 1984; Thomae, 1976). Data from these studies provided a way to test many of the theories and to describe the course of personality in adulthood.

Defining Adult Development

The major difference between theories of child development and adult development is that the former generally try to account for well-known phenomena; the latter try to point out phenomena to be explained. No one doubts that children acquire language at a tremendous rate; the theories concern whether language acquisition can be explained by operant conditioning, modeling, deep structure, or other processes. By contrast, there is a good deal of doubt whether adults experience meaningful changes around midlife, or whether older adults develop wisdom.

In fact, lay conceptions of aging are full of contradictions. We believe that people mellow with age—and also that they become cranky. We recognize the infirmities of age and then contend that old people are merely hypochondriacs. We attribute both wisdom and senility to the elderly. We speak of old age as the "golden years," but we believe that most older people suffer from depression and fear of death.

Theories of adult development, therefore, cannot be explanations of acknowledged facts but must disclose patterns previously unnoticed. Piaget's observation that the cognitive errors of children are not random mistakes but the products of a consistent, if imperfect, logic was the basis for some of the most important research in child development. In the same way, clinicians (Gould, 1978) and researchers who intensively studied small samples (Levinson et al., 1978) hoped to let new patterns emerge. It is, however, somewhat disconcerting to notice that different thinkers have pointed to very different phenomena as constituting the core of adult development. Erikson's generativity pulls the individual out of him- or herself into concern for the larger social structure; Levinson's midlife transition seems to emphasize increasing individuality. Disengagement theory (Cumming & Henry, 1961) was challenged by activity theory (Maddox, 1963). The view that older people adopt more primitive modes of defense (Pfeiffer, 1977) conflicts with the view that styles of coping and defense mature with age (Vaillant, 1977).

If these theoretical postions were merely competing hypotheses, it would be relatively easy to decide among them empirically. In most cases, however, they point to different levels of analysis: Neugarten (1964), for instance, suggested that there may be stability in socioadaptational processes and development in intrapsychic processes. Perhaps the most difficult problem facing advocates of adult development theories is simply defining the field of study. Should we focus on ego styles, interpersonal behaviors, facial expressions of emotion, social support networks, life stories, or life structures? What exactly would adult development be the development of? Few biologists would use the term *development* to describe the physical changes that occur with aging: the decline of sensory and motor functions, the increased susceptibility to illness, the loss of recuperative powers. But adulthood is very different when viewed by the sociologist, who sees careers wax and wane, historical changes engulf the individual, and family roles change.

There is an obvious sense in which adult life is structured by social conventions (which in turn are based in part in biology). Young adults marry, take on economic burdens, raise children. White-collar and professional workers expect to advance in their careers, and economic and social power resides in the hands of the middle-aged (Neugarten, 1968). Children leave home and parents die, then retirement and grandparenting loom, then perhaps widowhood. With many cultural and subcultural variants, this basic pattern recurs, and it makes a reasonable framework for a life-cycle approach to sociology. There is, however, no particular reason to describe it as "development". Adult development enters when these changes affect the psychology of the individual—when the person adapts and grows with experience.

In recent years there has been increasing attention to the study of lives through psychobiography and life narratives (Levinson et al., 1978; McAdams & Ochberg, 1988; Runyan, 1980), which might seem to offer the best hope for charting adult development. Levinson and his colleagues, in fact, consider adult development to be the orderly transitions of the *life structure*, a hybrid concept intended to integrate both the inner psychology of the individual and the social network in which he or she is embedded at any given time. There is no doubt that individuals interact with their social environment over time to produce a unique life course— just as character and dramatic conflict unfold over time to form the plot of a play. There is also no doubt that the study of lives is and should be a major concern for personality psychologists (White, 1964).

What is not clear is whether this is a good approach to use in the study of adult development. Psychological reconstructions are always problematic (Ross & Conway, 1986; Runyan, 1981), and the use of life narratives as the basis for building a psychology of adult development is particularly perilous. Lives change over time, but do these changes affect the person? Do they follow discernible patterns, or are they random perturbations, unique to a historical era (Gergen, 1977)? Fascinating as psychobiography may be, we believe it should be informed by studies of adult development, not vice versa. If we understand how people change as they age—if at all—we will be in a much better position to interpret the course of an individual's life.

We are left, then, with the conclusion that adult development should be viewed as the development not of social roles, or life structures, but of personality. Yet this refocusing does not resolve the problem, given the wide array of definitions of personality. Should we be concerned with aggressive and sexual instincts and their viscissitudes, or with personal constructs, or mechanisms of coping and defense, or manifest needs, or cognitive styles, or self-concept, or locus of control?

Empirical Strategies

It might seem obvious that research should be guided by theory: We should select for study those personality variables that we have a reason to expect will show meaningful change. There have been many examples of this kind of research. Whitbourne and Waterman (1979) used a measure of Erikson psychosocial development and found some of the predicted changes in subjects who had been out of college for 10 years. Vaillant and colleagues (Vaillant, 1977; Vaillant & Drake, 1985; Vaillant, Bond, & Vaillant, 1986) have conducted a series of studies to evaluate a theory of maturation in mechanisms of defense. Loevinger's sentence completion measure of ego development has also been used in adult samples, although these studies have not found age-related increases in ego level (McCrae & Costa, 1980; Vaillant & McCullough, 1987).

Theory-based research is clearly an important direction for the field, but it is not the only one. Theories of aging rarely have well-validated measures associated with them, and they are correspondingly difficult to test. In addition, there is no guarantee that theorists have attended to the right aspects of personality. Important changes may be going on that have thus far escaped notice. Exploratory empirical research is a much-needed supplement to theory testing—provided it is systematic.

It is very easy to conduct a cross-sectional study of age-related differences in personality: Choose a measure and administer it to young and older subjects. Although it requires more patience, doing a longitudinal study of personality requires very little more thought: Choose a measure and administer it to the same subjects twice, after a lapse of sufficient time. What is difficut is to describe age-related differences or changes in personality systematically, because this implies that the researcher has a conception of personality that is meaningful, measurable, and comprehensive in scope. Models and measures of personality thus become paramount concerns for those studying adult development.

The basic unit of analysis we have adopted is the trait, a dimension of psychological functioning that can be used to differentiate and thus characterize individuals. Traits identify relatively enduring dispositions in individuals, characteristic ways of thinking, feeling, and acting; they are basic emotional, interpersonal, experiential, attitudinal, and motivational styles. Many personality psychologists prefer another level of analysis as a basis for theory, but most utilize trait measures for purposes of description. Whether personality is held to be a matter of learning, heredity, unconscious processes, or social roles, it is manifest in characteristic patterns that can be called traits.

Trait psychology thus offers a conception of personality that is both meaningful and measurable (Costa & McCrae, 1980b; Hogan, DeSoto, & Solano, 1977), but is it comprehensive? There are thousands of English-language trait names (Allport & Odbert, 1936) and hundreds of inventories that measure thousands of proposed traits; together, these two sources are likely to provide a comprehensive survey of important differences in normal personality. The problem is to find a way to organize these traits into a manageable number of groups (or *domains*) that still represent the full range of personality variables.

Fortunately, the past decade has seen widening acceptance of a taxonomy of personality traits, specifically, of the five-factor model (Digman & Inouye, 1986; Hogan, 1983; John, Goldberg, & Angleitner, 1984; McCrae & Costa, 1985b, 1987; Norman, 1963; Tupes & Christal, 1961). Studies using self-reports and peer ratings on questionnaires, Q-sorts, and adjective checklists in English, German, and other languages have repeatedly shown that the five broad dimensions of Neuroticisim, Extraversion, Openness to Experience, Agreeableness, and Conscientiousness underlie most of the traits used both in natural language and in professional assessment. Examples of adjectives that characterize the five factors are given in Table 1.

Our approach to the study of adult development thus begins with the description of stability and change in traits from each of the five domains. When complete, such a description tells us the ways in which individuals differ in their characteristic ways of thinking, feeling, and acting as a function of their age or maturational experience. Clearly, the findings would have considerable relevance for many theories of adult development: Are there clear demarcations between personality traits before and after age 40? Do traits suppressed in youth emerge in later life? Do older men show feminine traits? Does introversion increase with age? Does rigidity? Wisdom? It is true that the trait measures we examine here were not, in general, developed to test theories of aging specifically, but it seems reasonable to expect theories of aging to address stability or change in these measures. We submit that the body of evidence on personality traits in adulthood should form the starting point for conceptions of adult development.

Enduring Dispositions in Adulthood

When Does Adulthood Begin?

In order to review the literature on personality in adulthood, we must give at least a preliminary definition of that period of life. Legal definitions of adulthood vary widely, not only by state, but by function. A woman is legally of an age to marry at 14 in many states; the driver's license—that adolescent rite of passage—is withheld until age 16, voting until age 18, and drinking until age 21. Insurance companies, with actuarial wisdom, charge higher rates for drivers under 25. William James and a generation of hippies set age 30 as the dividing point between youth and settled adulthood.

Most psychologists probably consider college students—at least by the time of graduation—to be full-fledged adults. In many respects, of course, they are. There is reason to think, however, that personality development continues, at least for some individuals, for several more years. Researchers who trace individuals from college age into later adulthood almost invariably report some changes in mean levels of personality variables and lower levels of retest stability than are found in studies of individuals who are initially older (Finn, 1986; Helson & Moane, 1987; Jessor, 1983; Mortimer, Finch, & Kumka, 1982). Haan, Millsap, and Hartka (1986) concluded from a study of Q-sort-rated

Table 1
Characteristics Describing Five Personality Traits

Neuroticism
    Calm–Worrying
    Even-tempered–Temperamental
    Self-satisfied–Self-pitying
    Comfortable–Self-conscious
    Unemotional–Emotional
    Hardy–Vulnerable

Extraversion
    Reserved–Affectionate
    Loner–Joiner
    Quiet–Talkative
    Passive–Active
    Sober–Fun-loving
    Unfeeling–Passionate

Openness
    Down-to-earth–Imaginative
    Uncreative–Creative
    Conventional–Original
    Prefer routine–Prefer variety
    Uncurious–Curious
    Conservative–Liberal

Agreeableness
    Ruthless–Soft-hearted
    Suspicious–Trusting
    Stingy–Generous
    Antagonistic–Acquiescent
    Critical–Lenient
    Irritable–Good-natured

Conscientiousness
    Negligent–Conscientious
    Lazy–Hard-working
    Disorganized–Well-organized
    Late–Punctual
    Aimless–Ambitious
    Quitting–Persevering

Note. Data are based on Costa and McCrae (1985b).

personality that important changes in personality may occur after high school: "Great shifts in personality organization are ordinarily thought to occur *during* adolescence, but these findings suggest that more marked shifts occur, not during adolescence, but at its end when most people make the profound role shifts entailed by entry into full-time work and marriage" (p. 225). Such findings constitute a mandate for studying personality development in the decade of the 20s.

If we define adulthood as the period from age 18 on, studies like these make it clear that there is indeed adult development in aspects of personality. And if personality change continued to be the rule throughout the life span, chronological age would be the only reasonable basis for defining adulthood. As we will show, however, there is considerable evidence suggesting that the process of personality change as a normative, maturational phenomenon does not continue at a perceptible pace after age 30 or so. Somewhere in the decade between 20 and 30, individuals attain a configuration of traits that will characterize them for years to come. From the perspective of a trait psychologist, adulthood begins at that point.

Two Kinds of Change in Personality Traits

In principle, there are many possible ways in which traits might change over the life span: means, variances, reliabilities, or correlates might be the focus of research on personality and aging. In fact, however, the great majority of studies have been concerned with mean level changes and retest stability, partially because these are the most basic ways of addressing the issue, and partially because attempts to look for other kinds of change have not provided promising leads (e.g., McCrae, Costa, & Arenberg, 1980).

Mean level and retest stability are conceptually and statistically independent. An examination of mean levels in different age groups or at different times can tell the investigator about the extent and direction of general maturational trends. For example, a comparison of college and adult norms on the NEO Personality Inventory (NEO-PI; Costa & McCrae, 1985) suggests that adults in general score lower than do students on measures of Neuroticism, Extraversion, and Openness (Costa & McCrae, 1989). In the years following college, most individuals appear to become a bit calmer, quieter, and less curious. The hundreds of cross-sectional studies of age and personality reviewed by Neugarten (1977) and later by Bengston, Reedy, and Gordon (1985) all address this basic issue: Do older people score higher or lower than do younger people on some trait measure?

If the group as a whole shifts in mean level over time, we know that at least some individuals must be changing. The converse is not necessarily true: It is possible that each individual changes dramatically over the life span without any change in the average level of an age group, provided that the increases in some individuals are matched by decreases in others. This seesaw pattern is not merely a statistical oddity—it is a direct prediction from the Jungian premise that individuals should develop in later life qualities that they lacked in youth. Young extraverts would then become old introverts, and vice versa.

It is impossible to test this hypothesis with cross-sectional data. When longitudinal data are available over a reasonable interval of time, the retest correlation, or stability coefficient, gives an indication of how well the rank ordering of individuals is maintained. High correlations indicate that those who initially score high on the trait still score high compared to their peers at the second administration. The seesaw pattern would be suggested by correlations that became smaller with time and significantly negative after the passage of many years. Note that stability coefficients are not affected by changes in the mean level. This is seen in IQ scores of schoolchildren, who increase dramatically in intellectual capacity from 1st to 12th grade, but preserve their class standing over the same period. A high retest correlation would be seen here.

Age Differences and Changes in Mean Levels of Traits

There have been hundreds of cross-sectional studies comparing different age groups on the level of a wide variety of personality traits. Individually, many of them have shown significant effects. Collectively, however, it is much less clear that any pattern of results has emerged. Small differences in isolated studies are likely to be due to sampling biases. For example, college students may be compared to community-dwelling adults who have less than a college education. Differences in health status are also frequent and might account for some findings. Neugarten's (1977) review led her to conclude that there may be small decreases in Extraversion, but that other personality variables did not seem to change systematically with age.

A recent study on a national sample of almost 10,000 individuals aged 35 to 84 provides support for this view (Costa et al., 1986). Respondents were part of a follow-up study of a panel originally interviewed by the National Center for Health Statistics in 1971 and 1975. Ten years later, about two thirds of the sample were relocated, alive, and willing to participate. Among many other items, they were given brief scales to measure Neuroticism, Extraversion, and Openness to Experience. When plotted by decade, it is clear that there was very little effect of age on any of the three dimensions for men or women, Blacks or Whites (see Figure 1). As Neugarten suggested, there is a statistically significant decline in Extraversion—but it is so small that age accounts for less than 3 percent of the variance. There are also small declines in Neuroticism and in Openness. Note that the decline in Neuroticism contradicts popular

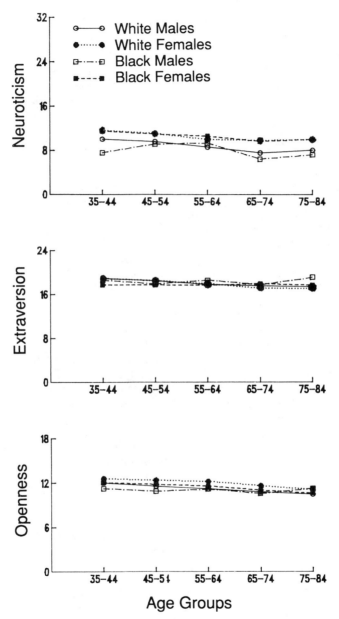

Figure 1. Mean levels of Neuroticism, Extraversion, and Openness to Experience for 10-year age groups of White men, Black men, White women, and Black women, aged 35 to 84 years. Data are derived from Costa et al. (1986).

stereotypes that suggest that old age is a period of depression and hypochondriasis.

Even these small effects might be the result of generational differences rather than of maturational changes. For example, individuals born early in the century might have been raised to be more conventional and conservative and thus have scored lower on Openness to Experience. Longitudinal studies, in which subjects serve as their own controls, avoid these problems of cohort difference, as well as other sampling biases.

A number of longitudinal studies have been used to examine changes in the mean levels of personality variables in adults (Bray & Howard, 1983; Costa & McCrae, 1978, 1988; Douglas & Arenberg, 1978; Leon, Gillum, Gillum, & Gouze, 1979; Siegler, George, & Okun, 1979), and most have reported predominant stability of mean levels. Siegler and her colleagues examined age changes on the Sixteen Personality Factor Questionnaire (16PF) in a sample of 331 men and women born between 1899 and 1922. Subjects were assessed 4 times over an 8-year period, and repeated measures analyses were conducted for each of the 16 scales. Intellectual brightness increased over time—probably due to practice on the test—and Guilt-proneness showed a Time × Sex interaction, with men decreasing and women increasing in scores on this scale, but there were no changes in the other 14 scales. The authors concluded that "the results indicate little evidence of significant differences across cohorts, changes over time, or their interaction" (Siegler et al., 1979, p. 351). Similarly, when Douglas and Arenberg (1978) examined the 10 scales of the Guilford–Zimmerman Temperament Scales (GZTS) in a 7-year longitudinal study of 336 men initially aged 20 to 81, they found significant changes in 5 of the scales, but further analyses suggested that only 2 of the scales—General Activity and Masculinity—showed patterns of change that appeared to be maturational. Even these changes were quite small in magnitude, amounting to only about one eighth of a standard deviation over the 7 years of the study. Although the results of this study seem to support the view that men become increasingly feminized with age, the rate of change is so slow that the typical Baltimore Longitudinal Study of Aging (BLSA) man would have to live to the age of 211 to score as low on Masculinity as college women did (Costa, McCrae, & Arenberg, 1983).

In addition to cross-sectional and longitudinal studies of mean levels, there is a third design that can sometimes be used: the cross-sequential design with independent samples (Baltes, 1968; Schaie, 1977). In this approach two groups of people, who were born at the same time but tested at different times, are compared. For example, one group might have been born in 1910 and tested in 1960, when they were 50 years old; the second group would be tested in 1980 when they were 70 years old. Any differences between the two groups could not be due to birth cohort effects, because both were born and raised in the same period. Furthermore, the cross-sequential design avoids any practice or memory effects that might be introduced when testing the same individuals twice.

This design was used by Douglas and Arenberg, and also by us as part of a recent study (Costa & McCrae, 1988) using the NEO-PI. Cross-sequential analyses of data from 1,143 men and women tested in 1980 or 1986 showed small increases in Extraversion and Openness, but no change in Neuroticism. These findings appear directly to contradict the cross-sectional results portrayed in Figure 1, in which all three of these domains declined with age. The explanation seems to be that there were general historical changes over the retest interval—subtle shifts in the meaning of the items or in prevailing attitudes. These time-of-measurement effects were detected when a different analysis, the time-sequential design, was used. The same phenomenon seems to account for cross-sequential declines in Agreeableness and Conscientiousness seen over a three-year period in the same study. Taken together, these analyses support the conclusion that there is little or no change in the mean levels of traits in any of the five domains of personality in adulthood.

Maturation is not a variable that can be manipulated; consequently, all studies of maturational change are quasi-experimental (Schaie, 1977) and can never be interpreted unambiguously. But all study designs—cross-sectional, longitudinal, cross-sequential, and others—do provide data that can form the basis of an informed judgment (Costa & McCrae, 1982). A comparison of available data from many designs supports the view that most personality variables neither increase nor decrease much for most people across the adult life span.

These findings are of great importance in understanding the course of normal aging. Age is only weakly related to personality traits; attempts to describe periods of life in terms of characteristic dispositions are therefore unlikely to succeed. Stereotypes that depict older men and women as depressed, withdrawn, rigid, and cranky are without empirical foundation. Adults of all ages show a wide range of individual differences, and these differences are likely to be more important in predicting well-being, coping, and interpersonal relations than is age.

Stability of Individual Differences

Are individual differences stable, or do they shift randomly or systematically over time? Different theoretical perspectives lead to different predictions. Freud believed that, without the aid of psychoanalysis, individual character was fixed in childhood. Erikson's epigenetic model recognized the possibility of change at each period of the life span. Role theorists who see personality in terms of the self-concept and tie it to changing social roles are likely to predict change, as would social learning theorists and life stress researchers, who hold that personality should be continuously reshaped by changing contingencies and traumatic events. Marriage and divorce, wars and depressions, chronic illnesses, and endless hours of working on a factory line or watching television have a tremendous impact on individuals' lives; it seems axiomatic that they would also affect people's personalities.

Cross-sectional studies tell us nothing about the stability of traits in the individual. Retrospective studies—in which individuals are asked to recall their earlier personality and subsequent changes—are questionable, because memory is easily distorted by current concerns and beliefs (Ross & Conway, 1986). Still, it is of some interest to consider retrospective findings as a hint of what longitudinal research may show. A classic study by Reichard et al. (1962) included careful reconstructions of the past and led to the conclusion that "the histories of our aging workers suggest that their personality characteristics changed very little throughout their lives" (p. 163). Those who anticipate major changes in personality over the life span may well dismiss such conclusions by attributing them to the distortion of memory, so it is imperative that more objective evidence be sought.

Only longitudinal designs, in which the same individuals are assessed at two or more time points, can provide good evidence on this point. The most useful metric for measuring stability is the retest correlation, or stability coefficient. Note that this is calculated in the same way as a retest reliability coefficient, a fact that serves as a reminder that stability coefficients are limited, or attenuated, by the reliability of the measures involved. When instruments with low reliability, like the Thematic Apperception Test (TAT), are used, stability coefficients in the range of .2 to .4 may be seen (Skolnick, 1966). What happens when more reliable measures are used?

Table 2 summarizes the major longitudinal studies of personality stability reported in the past decade. The studies employed a wide range of personality measures, samples, and retest intervals, but all show a similar pattern of results. Regardless of the instrument or sample, there is evidence of substantial stability in personality over intervals of up to 30 years. Median correlations from the studies range from .34 to .75, with most above .50. Although there is wide variation both within and across studies in the stability coefficients for different scales, there is no doubt that there is substantial stability in individual rank-order for adults.

In general, it appears that higher stability is evident in studies in which subjects are initially over age 30. After this point, however, increasing age does not lead to increasing stability (Costa, McCrae, & Arenberg, 1980), as theories of increasing interiority had predicted (Neugarten, 1964). In our study of NEO-PI scales (Costa & McCrae, 1988), we examined 6-year stability coefficients for traits in the domains of Neuroticism, Extraversion, and Openness to Experience separately for men and women initially aged 25 to 56 and 57 to 84. With median correlations for the four groups ranging from .69 to .74, there was no evidence of higher stability for older subjects.

Several authors have suggested that there is a gradual decline in stability coefficients with longer retest intervals (Conley, 1984; Schuerger, Tait, & Tavernelli, 1982). The median stability coefficient over a 6-year interval for 114 men on GZTS scales was .77; this declined to .74 over a 12-year interval (Costa et al., 1980). Leon et al.'s (1979) MMPI data, as shown in Table 2, also show a drop in median correlation from .50 for 13 years to .40 for 30 years. By contrast, Stevens and Truss (1985) show larger stability coefficients for subjects who were retested after 20 years than for those retested after 12 years (see Table 2). This is an issue that remains to be resolved, but it is clear that there is substantial stability even for very long intervals and that any decline with time is small by comparison.

In order to understand the true stability of personality, retest coefficients must be examined relative to retest reliability. After all, if test scores fluctuate widely over a 2-week interval, they cannot be expected to show much stability over 20 years. When statistical corrections are made to disattenuate stability coefficients for unreliability, many of the correlations approach unity, suggesting that if measures were perfectly reliable, near-perfect stability would be seen (Costa & McCrae, 1988; Costa et al., 1980).

A final point about the data in Table 2 concerns the generalizability of stability across dimensions of personality. The majority of scales included in Table 2 measure aspects of either Neuroticism or Extraversion, both of which are widely held to be temperamental dimensions, with substantial heritability (Finn, 1986). What about Openness, Agreeableness, and Conscientiousness, dimensions that may be more susceptible to the influences of experience and socialization? With respect to Openness, there is now solid evidence that it shows a level of stability comparable to that seen for Neuroticism and Extraversion, with a 6-year retest coefficient of .83 for total Openness on the NEO-PI (Costa & McCrae, 1988). Evidence on Agreeableness and Conscientiousness is more prelminary, but a similar level of stability is suggested.

All of the data in Table 2 are derived from self-reports. Although the validity of self-reports as a source of psychological information has been strongly affirmed in recent years (McCrae, 1982b; Shrauger & Osberg, 1981), self-reports should not form the only line of evidence on stability or change in personality. It could be argued that the self-concept, on which the individual draws in answering the questions of a personality inventory, becomes crystallized at some point; the individual would then be incapable of perceiving or reporting change even if it occurred (Rosenberg, 1979). Both cross-sectional (McCrae & Costa, 1982) and longitudinal (Costa & McCrae, 1988) comparisons with ratings by spouses lead us to reject this hypothesis. The self-concept may become crystallized, but only because personality itself does.

Table 2

Stability Coefficients for Recent Longitudinal Studies Using Self-Report Instruments

Study	Instrument	N	Sex	Initial Age	Retest Interval	Correlations	
						Range	Median
Block (1977)	CPI	219	M,F	31–38	10		.71
Costa & McCrae (1978)	16PF	139	M	25–82	10	.24–.64	.50
Siegler et al. (1979)	16PF	331	M,F	45–70	2		.50
Leon et al. (1979)	MMPI	71	M	45–54	13	.07–.82	.50
				58–67	17	.03–.76	.52
				45–54	30	.28–.74	.40
Costa et al. (1980)	GZTS	60	M	20–44	12	.61–.85	.72
		87	M	45–59	12	.64–.85	.75
		32	M	60–76	12	.59–.87	.73
Mortimer et al. (1982)	Self-concept	368	M	Seniors	10	.51–.63	.55
Conley (1985a)	KLS Factors	378	M,F	18–35	20	.34–.57	.46
Howard & Bray[1]	EPPS	266	M	Young Managers	20	.31–.54	.42
	GAMIN	264	M		20	.45–.61	.57

(table continued)

Table 2 (continued)

Study	Instrument	N	Sex	Initial Age	Retest Interval	Correlations	
						Range	Median
Stevens & Truss (1985)	EPPS	85	M,F	College Students	12	−.05–.58	.34
		92	M,F		20	−.01–.79	.44
Finn (1986)	MMPI Factors	96	M	17–25	30	−.14–.58	.35
		78	M	43–53	30	.10–.88	.56
Helson & Moane (1987)	CPI	81	F	21	22	.21–.58	.37
				27	16	.40–.70	.51
	ACL	78	F	27	16	.49–.72	.61
Costa & McCrae (1988)	NEO-PI	234	M	25–84	6	.60–.87	.74
		164	F	25–84	6	.58–.85	.73

Note. CPI = California Psychological Inventory; 16PF = Sixteen Personality Factor Questionnaire; MMPI = Minnesota Multiphasic Personality Inventory; GZTS = Guilford–Zimmerman Temperament Survey; KLS = Kelly Longitudinal Study; EPPS = Edwards Personal Preference Schedule; GAMIN = Guilford/Martin Inventory of Factors; ACL = Adjective Check List; NEO-PI = NEO Personality Inventory.
[1] A. Howard & D. W. Bray (personal communication, May 10, 1985).

Perhaps the most direct way to demonstrate this is by an examination of longitudinal stability in rated personality. Table 3 gives retest correlations for men and women rated by spouses; the data are virtually identical to those from self-reports. Husbands and wives continue to describe their spouses in the same ways at least over a period of six years. These findings are consistent with the pioneering work of Block (Block with Haan, 1971), who used Q-sorts from expert raters to trace children from junior high school through senior high and into early adulthood. Block demonstrated both change and continuity in rated personality over this long and formative period. Haan et al., (1986) continued this research into middle age and reported stability coefficients for Q-sort components, which ranged from .24 to .64 for the period of early to middle adulthood and from .25 to .74 for middle to late adulthood. Considering that

Table 3
Retest Correlations for Men and Women Rated by Spouses

NEO-PI Scale	Men ($n = 89$)	Women ($n = 78$)	Total ($N = 167$)
Neuroticism	.77	.86	.83
Anxiety	.67	.82	.75
Hostility	.76	.81	.78
Depression	.69	.74	.72
Self-Consciousness	.65	.77	.76
Impulsiveness	.70	.81	.75
Vulnerability	.62	.70	.68
Extraversion	.78	.77	.77
Warmth	.76	.70	.75
Gregariousness	.71	.72	.73
Assertiveness	.68	.75	.72
Activity	.72	.63	.68
Excitement Seeking	.65	.75	.69
Positive Emotions	.78	.77	.77
Openness	.82	.78	.80
Fantasy	.73	.73	.73
Aesthetics	.83	.70	.79
Feelings	.71	.65	.70
Actions	.78	.69	.75
Ideas	.75	.72	.75
Values	.81	.72	.76

Note. NEO-PI = NEO Personality Inventory. All correlations are significant at $p < .001$. Adapted from Costa & McCrae (1988) by permission.

personality ratings were made by different judges at different periods—which means that true change was confounded with method variance introduced by different observers—this is strong evidence for stability.

Self-Perceived Change in Personality

Many people find the assertion that there are few changes in adult personality counterintuitive: Their own experience convinces them that important changes occur. These convictions, of course, are subjective, based on the individuals' memories of what they were once like and their current view of themselves, and they may or may not be well founded. But self-perceptions of change (Gold, Andres, & Schwartzman, 1987; Ryff, 1982; Ryff & Heincke, 1983) are an interesting topic in themselves. Can they be used to identify a subgroup of individuals who actually change? Do they speak to the influence of age stereotypes on self-perceptions? Do they reflect systematic distortions in memory or strategies of self-presentation?

We conducted a small study of self-perceptions of personality change in conjunction with our six-year longitudinal study of self-reports and spouse ratings on the NEO-PI (Costa & McCrae, 1988). At the end of our packet of questionnaires, we asked subjects to "think back over the last six years to the way you were in 1980. Consider your basic feelings, attitudes, and ways of relating to people—your whole personality. Overall, do you think you have (a) changed a good deal in your personality? (b) changed a little in your personality? or (c) stayed pretty much the same in personality since 1980?" We found that a bare majority (51 percent) believed they had stayed "pretty much the same," and another third (35 percent) though they had changed "a little." But a substantial minority—14 percent—felt that they had changed significantly in personality. These individuals would probably take exception to our conclusions about personality stability.

Are these perceptions veridical, or are they distorted by tricks of perception or memory? One simple way to examine this question is by comparing stability coefficients within the three perceived change groups. If perceptions of change are accurate, they should be reflected in lower stability coefficients, both in self-reports and in spouse ratings. As Table 4 shows, however, none of the five personality factors is consistently less stable among individuals who believe they had changed "a good deal" in personality.

When perceived change was correlated with age, education, sex, and personality traits, the only substantial correlation was with age. Older individuals perceived less change ($r = -.27, N = 936, p < .001$), perhaps because they have adopted stereotypes of old age as a time of rigidity, or perhaps because older generations are less influenced by recent ideals

Table 4
Six-Year Stability Coefficients for NEO Personality Inventory Domain
Scales Within Perceived Change Groups

NEO-PI Scale	Perceived Change		
	"A good deal"	"A little"	"The same"
Self-reports			
Neuroticism	.77 (43)	.79 (148)	.86 (182)
Extraversion	.66 (43)	.80 (148)	.86 (182)
Openness	.86 (43)	.83 (148)	.82 (182)
Agreeableness[1]	.70 (36)	.56 (132)	.62 (173)
Conscientiousness[1]	.80 (36)	.71 (132)	.81 (173)
Spouse Ratings			
Neuroticism	.86 (13)	.79 (56)	.84 (71)
Extraversion	.79 (13)	.79 (56)	.72 (71)
Openness	.90 (13)	.88 (56)	.71 (71)
Median	.80	.79	.82

*Note. n*s are given within parentheses. All correlations are significant at $p < .01$.
[1]Three-year stability coefficients based on preliminary scales.

of continuing adult development. Alternatively, long experience may have taught older individuals to perceive the stability in their own personality.

It is possible that a single item assessing global change is too imprecise to offer a meaningful test of the accuracy of perceived change. To assess perceived changes in Extraversion, therefore, we also asked subjects "specifically, compared to how you were six years ago, how lively, cheerful, and sociable are you now?" Parallell items asked about the other four dimensions, and subjects could respond with "more," "less," or "same."

Although the majority of responses (54 percent) suggested perceived stability, many individuals reported changes in one or more dimensions. Older subjects were more likely than younger subjects to report that they had become lower in Extraversion, Openness, and particularly Conscientiousness, perhaps reflecting stereotypes of the aging process. Men and women apparently shared the same perceptions; there were no Age × Gender interactions in perceived change (cf. Ryff & Heincke, 1983).

For those subjects with longitudinal self-reports or spouse ratings, it was again possible to test the veridicality of these perceptions by analyzing questionnaire data. Repeated measures analyses of variance were conducted on each NEO-PI domain score, with individuals classified according to their perceived change on that domain. The Time ×

Perceived Change interaction term in these analyses is of chief interest here: Do individuals who claim to have beome more extraverted actually increase in Extraversion scores relative to those who believe they have stayed the same or become more introverted?

Consistent with this hypothesis, small but significant effects were found for both Neuroticism and Extraversion in the expected direction when self-reports were examined. Neither effect was replicated, however, when spouse ratings were analyzed, so some bias in self-reports might be suspected. Perhaps those individuals who reported that they had become more "anxious, upset, or unhappy" over the past six years were experiencing a transient period of stress or depression that contributed to an elevated Neuroticism score. There was no evidence that perceived changes in Openness, Agreeableness, or Conscientiousness corresponded to measured changes.

The overall direction of perceived changes suggested that another systematic bias was also operating. Of those who reported changes, 69 percent felt they were now lower in Neuroticism; 78 percent felt they were more "curious, open-minded, and imaginative," and 73 percent felt they were more "helpful, sympathetic, and trusting." It appears from this that individuals perceive themselves to have grown and become better adjusted with the passage of time.

Woodruff and Birren (1972) reported a similar finding in an ingenious study of objective and subjective age changes. A group of students had been given the California Test of Personality in 1944. Twenty-five years later the test was readministered to assess objective change in personality; in addition, however, subjects were asked to complete the questionnaire as they recalled having completed it 25 years earlier. Differences between the recalled 1944 data and the actual 1944 data gave an index of subjective age change. There were no significant changes in objectively measured personality, but there were substantial differences in subjective perceptions of personality: "Adults scored significantly lower when they described themselves as students than they had actually scored when they were students 25 years previously. They projected a negative picture of themselves back in time" (p. 255).

Although most adults see themselves as basically stable in personality (cf. Gold et al., 1987), many perceive changes in themselves. When these perceptions are tested against objective data, however, they find little or no support. For the most part, it appears that self-perceived changes in personality are misperceptions.

Possibilities for Change, Implications of Stability

No one proposes that personality is immutable. But the evidence for stability from longitudinal studies using different samples, measures, and methods is certainly remarkable, particularly in contrast to the expectations raised by theories of personality and adult development and by individuals' own retrospective perceptions of change. Dozens of theories compete to predict the course of transitions in adulthood, but the most compelling data point to continuity, despite role changes, traumatic events, biological aging, and the sheer accumulation of experience.

It is possible that we have failed to find patterns of growth because we have examined the wrong variables? Certainly there are many psychological variables that would not be considered personality traits. Moods, for example, are states, not traits, but research on psychological well-being (measured as the balance of negative and positive moods) shows little relation between mood and age (Costa et al., 1987). We found no systematic evidence of age-related differences in the perceptual variables measured by the Holtzman Inkblot Test (Costa & McCrae, 1986a), nor in ego level as measured by sentence completions (McCrae & Costa, 1982). Vaillant (1977) has reported finding maturation of defenses between college age and early adulthood, but studies of ways of coping in adults have shown that the great majority of coping strategies were used equally by adults of all ages (Lazarus & Delongis, 1982; McCrae, 1982a).

Predictable age-related changes can be found if the measures and concepts are tailored to changes in adulthood. For example, there are regular changes in the proportion of individuals who consider themselves middle-aged versus old or elderly (Bultena & Powers, 1978). Age identification, however, seems to be a relatively minor issue for most adults, and it is rarely mentioned as part of the spontaneous self-concept (McCrae & Costa, 1988). Adults of different ages doubtless differ in their current concerns, because these are dictated in part by changing life circumstances. And there is evidence that time orientation changes with age: From middle age on, people begin to think in terms of time left to live, rather than of time lived (Neugarten, 1968). The significance of this new perspective on time is not clear. It apparently does not lead to changes in fundamental emotional, social, or motivational styles.

There would seem to be two directions in which the study of adult development might proceed: It might be restricted to the period between 20 and 30, when changes are observed, or to the study of special samples, including individuals undergoing psychotherapy, in whom change might be expected; it might redefine the field as the psychology of adulthood, in which enduring dispositions would be viewed as a foundation for adaptation to the changing demands of life. We believe that both of these approaches are useful—researchers should study change where it occurs and stability where it does not. Psychotherapy, in particular, remains an area in which much remains to be done. Longitudinal studies are observational, not experimental: They tell us what happens to a sample of people during the normal course of events. The fact that most people do not change a great deal does not necessarily mean that they could not change given the right set of circumstances, and psychotherapy is likely to be a source of such change. The recently renewed interest in psychotherapy research (VandenBos, 1986) may provide an incentive for long-term, large-scale studies of the effects of different forms of therapy on personality. Conversely, findings of stability help put the therapeutic enterprise into perspective (Costa & McCrae, 1986b): Therapists and their clients should understand that there are powerful forces for continuity and that even modest improvements in basic dispositions may be a substantial achievement.

Toward a Psychology of Adulthood

Adulthood as a Period of Stability

The data on the continuity of personality in adulthood suggest that models of continuing growth and development across the life span are probably not an accurate basis for understanding adults. Some individuals, in some ways, and under some conditions, may show meaningful changes in personality; as a general rule, however, stability is much more important. Basing theories of adulthood on unusual cases of change may be as inappropriate as basing theories of normal personality on investigations of psychopathology.

We are not, however, advocating a return to the view of adulthood that prevailed before the advent of life span developmental psychology. The evidence suggests two important differences. First, with regard to personality, maturation appears to continue through the decade of the 20s. Developmental psychologists need to continue their studies beyond high school, and even beyond college, in order to understand the forces that shape personality. Second, there is little or no evidence of a decline in personality with age. According to conventional wisdom, old age is a period of regression or deterioration, and there are certainly dramatic and tragic changes that can occur as a result of dementia. But for most older men and women, characteristic ways of functioning continue throughout life.

For the personality theorist, the impressive degree of stability seen in logitudinal studies over several decades suggests that human beings are less a product of their environment than many social scientists have imagined. People are not passive victims of life events, historical movements, or changing social roles. They maintain their distinctive characteristics in the face of all these forces. New theories of personality that address the origins and maintenance of personality within the individual are needed. Some beginnings have already been made in this area: Caspi, Elder, and Bem (1987), for example, describe processes of cumulative and interactional continuity that help perpetuate some personality characteristics.

There are also important social policy implications. Both disengagement theory (Cumming & Henry, 1961) and activity theory (Maddox, 1963) have been used as models for designing social programs for the elderly, on the assumption that older people in general would benefit from reduced or increased social interaction. The difficulty with these positions is that they assume that older people are all alike, when in fact they are as different from each other as younger adults are. Opportunities for social activities will be relished by older extraverts, but not by older introverts, who might benefit more from a bookmobile program. Social programs should offer a wide range of options and services and allow older individuals to select those most in keeping with their own needs and dispositions.

Finally, stability of personality has implications for the individual. Enduring dispositions provide one of the foundations for a sense of identity and a basis for conducting our lives. Planning for a career, marriage, or retirement should be based on realistic projections of our needs, abilities, and styles, and the continuity of personality allows us to use the current self as a reliable indicator of the future self. Knowledge that social and emotional characteristics remain intact with age should be comforting to individuals who fear old age as a period of isolation and depression. And for those persons who are dissatisfied with aspects of their personality, the importance of psychotherapy or other active efforts to change should be clear: Aging itself is not likely to bring improvements.

Should employers plan to accommodate slackened productivity around the age of the midlife crisis? Should children expect their parents to mellow with age? Should psychotherapists prepare for an epidemic of depression as the population ages? Probably not. One of the major functions of personality theory is to allow predictions of how different individuals will behave in different situations. The stability of traits means these predictions will have utility many years in advance.

The Future of Personality and Aging

For years, gerontologists sought to understand the ways in which aging and age-related events shaped adult personality. Personality stability might seem to signal a failure of this effort and an end to research on personality and aging. If personality does not change with age, why study it? The answer, we believe, is that personality is a key to several crucial issues in aging (Costa & McCrae, 1980b). By understanding individual differences, we can predict careers, life outcomes, and adjustment to the threats, losses, and challenges of adult life.

Using data from the Berkeley longitudinal studies, Elder and his colleagues (Caspi et al., 1987; Elder & Clipp, 1988; Elder, Liker, & Jaworski, 1984) have conducted a series of studies that examine the impact of personality and significant life experiences in shaping the life course.

Children with a history of tantrums who were rated as ill-tempered later showed disturbances in career and marriage, with a higher probability of downward occupational mobility and divorce (Caspi et al., 1987). The Great Depression of the 1930s was a stressful event for many, but those who were lower in emotional stability before the Depression showed the greatest impact in subsequent poor adjustment (Elder et al., 1984). Similarly, those combat veterans who had stress reactions after World War II had been characterized by higher levels of inadequacy and anxiety during adolescence (Elder & Clipp, 1988).

Conley (1985b) traced the couples who had participated in E. Lowell Kelly's pioneering longitudinal study—a study that had provided some of the first strong evidence of personality stability (Kelly, 1955). Conley used self-reports and ratings gathered in 1935 and 1955 to predict aspects of life in 1980 and found evidence of pervasive influences of personality. For example, men and women rated by peers in 1935 as being high in Neuroticism were more likely to have had an emotional disorder in the succeeding years; men rated as poor in impulse control (or Conscientiousness) were more likely to have become alcoholics. Conley sampled a number of variables that give a flavor of daily life in 1980 for these men and women. His intuitive types—whom we would describe as open to experience—had artistic hobbies and preferred to watch public television. His sensing types—those who were closed to experience—listed gardening, sewing, and cooking as hobbies, and they preferred to watch game shows. Philosophies of life were predicted by the two dimensions of Openness and Agreeableness.

Our own research at the Normative Aging Study in Boston and the Baltimore Longitudinal Study of Aging have also shown how personality can predict life outcomes. Psychological well-being can be estimated years in advance from knowledge of Neuroticism and Extraversion (Costa & McCrae, 1980a; 1984). Neuroticism scores gathered 10 years earlier predicted the occurrence of a midlife crisis (Costa & McCrae, 1980b), and Openness to Experience was prospectively related to career shifts for both men and women (McCrae & Costa, 1985a).

In all these cases, researchers have relied on archival data to explore the impact of personality on the life course, and only rarely have measures of all five domains of personality been available. What is needed is a systematic prospective study, in which all domains of personality would be measured from childhood through age 30 as predictor variables. The outcome variables might include physical and psychiatric health, style and success of marriage and parenting, vocational history, accommodation to life stresses, creative achievements, leisure-time pursuits, social activities, attitudes, and attitude changes. Ideally, spouses or whole families would be studied so that the interaction of different personality traits in interpersonal relationships could be studied. Prospective studies, particularly of the scope suggested, will require decades. In the meantime, it may be useful to begin to examine the life course concurrently and retrospectively in relation to personality traits. Several recent developments in personality psychology lend themselves to this approach.

Little (1983) has proposed a new unit for the analysis of personality in context, the *personal project*. A personal project is a set of acts intended to achieve a goal; they range from "getting a better job" to "overcoming my shyness" to "going to the ballet" (p. 293). Individuals appear to be able to list the projects that concern them at any given time quite easily, and they can then rate them on dimensions such as importance, difficulty, control, and absorption. One advantage of using personal projects as a unit of analysis is that they provide a much more detailed specification of the life structure at a single time, and one that is phenomenologically real to the individual. An occupational history that includes only type of work and dates of hiring, promotion, and firing misses the richness that can be drawn from an analysis of personal projects: Are job concerns central to life, or simply an economic necessity? Are tasks part of an ongoing career plan, or a series of discrete activities? Is the work pleasant or unpleasant, absorbing or dull, imposed or chosen?

A second advantage to using personal projects for analysis is that the dimensions on which they are rated can be averaged across a series of projects and related to personality variables. We might find that highly conscientious individuals felt their projects were within their control, that open people became deeply absorbed in their projects, that those high in Neuroticism were dissatisfied with their progress. These kinds of analyses help to spell out the implications of personality traits and their influence on life in more detail.

A second approach that, although not new, has recently witnessed a resurgence of interest, is that of using psychobiography and life narratives (McAdams & Ochberg, 1988; Runyan, 1980). As McAdams (1988) pointed out, these two are somewhat different. Psychobiography is the psychological interpretation of an individual life; life narratives—the stories people tell about their lives—may form part of the raw material from which psychobiographies are constructed, or they may form a subject for study in themselves.

We have argued that life histories should not be used as the basis of a psychology of adult development; rather, we think that knowledge about personality and its continuity in adulthood can form a basis for understanding lives. The psychodynamic approaches of Freud and Erikson have had a tremendous influence on the thinking of historians and literary critics as well as psychologists, because psychoanalytic formulations could be used to make sense of an individual's life course. The same benefit can be offered by trait psychology, which has a much stronger empirical basis. Historians, of course, generally cannot administer standardized personality questionnaires, but they can use the behavior patterns of a lifetime to estimate standing on dimensions of personality and then use these as a framework for interpreting the significant events of their subjects' lives (cf. Winter & Carlson, 1988).

Applied across many life stories, this approach could also be used to formulate a more general psychology of the life span. Are there typical patterns of life history, classes of lives that show similar plots: comedies, tragedies, melodramas? If so, are these plots determined in some way by the dispositions of the individuals telling their stories, as classical tragedy was predicated on the hero's hubris? Surely the individual's perception of his or her life as revealed in a life narrative will be colored by prevailing emotions and experiential styles. Whether the investigator is interested in the story a person tells or the life itself, enduring dispositions are likely to provide a valuable perspective.

The clinician's task is in some ways similar to that of the psychobiographer. He or she must listen to the client's problems in living and attempt to understand them in terms of history, current life structure, and personality. Sorting out the environmental and dispositional influences on behavior becomes crucial, because an intelligent approach to solving problems requires knowledge of their source. Should the client change jobs, or would she merely take her difficulties to a new place of employment? Who is at fault in a marital dispute, and are the differences something that can be changed or that must be accepted? Is an older person's depression a sign of organic disease or part of a longstanding pattern? Measures of personality and an understanding of the implications of personality traits for the life structure and life course can provide guidance.

Putting adulthood into perspective—seeing the larger pattern, the grand sweep—has proven to be extraordinarily difficult, in large part because the careers of researchers are so much shorter than those of the people and events they hope to study. How can we understand an event that takes 70 years if we have only 40 years in which to observe it? The answer, of course, is that we must piece it together from different sources: retrospective accounts, cross-sectional studies, longitudinal research tracing different cohorts through shorter segments of historical time. Add to this the problems of abstracting the individual from the social context and development from historical change, and the task appears overwhelming. It is therefore remarkably fortunate that, in a few decades, we have come to understand one basic fact: The personality dispositions that form an essential part of our unique identity endure across adulthood as formative influences on the life course. With this insight as an anchor, progress in understanding the psychology of adulthood should be even swifter in the next few decades.

References

Allport, G. W., & Odbert, H. S. (1936). Trait names: A psycholexical study. *Psychological Monographs, 47* (1, Whole No. 211).

Arenberg, D., & Robertson-Tchabo, E. A. (1977). Learning and memory. In J. E. Birren & K. W. Schaie (Eds.), *Handbook of the psychology of aging* (1st ed., pp. 421–449). New York: Van Nostrand Reinhold.

Baltes, P. B. (1968). Longitudinal and cross-sectional sequences in the study of age and generation effects. *Human Development, 11*, 145–171.

Bell, B., Rose, C. L., & Damon, A. (1972). The Normative International Journal of Aging Study: An interdisciplinary and longitudinal study of health and aging. *International Journal of Aging and Human Development, 3*, 5–17.

Bengtson, V. L., Reedy, M. N., & Gordon, C. (1985). Aging and self-conceptions: Personality processes and social contexts. In J. E. Birren & K. W. Schaie (Eds.), *Handbook of the psychology of aging* (2nd ed., pp. 544–593). New York: Van Nostrand Reinhold.

Block, J. (1977). Advancing the psychology of personality: Paradigmatic shift or improving the quality of research? In D. Magnusson & N. S. Endler (Eds.), *Personality at the crossroads: Current issues in interactional psychology* (pp. 37–64). Hillsdale, NJ: Erlbaum.

Block, J., with Haan, N. (1971). *Lives through time.* Berkeley, CA: Bancroft Books.

Bray, D. W., & Howard, A. (1983). The AT&T Longitudinal Studies of Managers. In K. W. Schaie (Ed.), *Longitudinal studies of adult psychological development* (pp. 266–312). New York: Guilford Press.

Bühler, C. (1935). The curve of life as studies in biographies. *Journal of Applied Psychology, 19*, 405–409.

Bultena, G. L., & Powers, E. A. (1978). Denial of aging: Age identification and reference group orientations. *Journal of Gerontology, 33*, 748–754.

Butler, R. N. (1963). The life review: An interpretation of reminiscence in the aged. *Psychiatry, 26*, 65–76.

Caspi, A., Elder, G. H., Jr., & Bem, D. J. (1987). Moving against the world: Life-course patterns of explosive children. *Developmental Psychology, 23*, 308–313.

Conley, J. J. (1984). The hierarchy of consistency: A review and model of longitudinal findings on adult individual differences in intelligence, personality, and self-opinion. *Personality and Individual Differences, 5*, 11–26.

Conley, J. J. (1985a). Longitudinal stability of personality traits: a multitrait-multimethod-multioccasion analysis. *Journal of Personality and Social Psychology, 49*, 1266–1282.

Conley, J. J. (1985b). A personality theory of adulthood and aging. In R. Hogan & W. H. Jones (Eds.), *Perspectives in personality* (Vol. 1, pp. 81–115). Greenwich, CT: JAI Press.

Constantinople, A. (1969). An Erikson measure of personality development in college students. *Developmental Psychology, 1*, 357–372.

Costa, P. T., Jr., & McCrae, R. R. (1978). Objective personality assessment. In M. Storandt, I. C. Siegler, & M. F. Elias (Eds.), *The clinical psychology of aging* (pp. 119–143). New York: Plenum Press.

Costa, P. T., Jr., & McCrae, R. R. (1980a). Influence of extraversion and neuroticism on subjective well-being: Happy and unhappy people. *Journal of Personality and Social Psychology, 38*, 668–678.

Costa, P. T., Jr., & McCrae, R. R. (1980b). Still stable after all these years: Personality as a key to some issues in adulthood and old age. In P. B. Baltes

& O. G. Brim, Jr. (Eds.), *Life span development and behavior* (Vol. 3, pp. 65–102). New York: Academic Press.

Costa, P. T., Jr., & McCrae, R. R. (1982). An approach to the attribution of age, period, and cohort effects. *Psychological Bulletin, 92*, 238–250.

Costa, P. T., Jr., & McCrae, R. R. (1984). Personality as a lifelong determinant of well-being. In C. Malatesta & C. Izard (Eds.), *Affective processes in adult development and aging* (pp. 141–157). Beverly Hills, CA: Sage.

Costa, P. T., Jr., & McCrae, R. R. (1985). *The NEO Personality Inventory manual.* Odessa, FL: Psychological Assessment Resources, Inc.

Costa, P. T., Jr., & McCrae, R. R. (1986a). Age, personality, and the Holtzman Inkblot Technique. *International Journal of Aging and Human Development, 23*, 115–125.

Costa, P. T., Jr., & McCrae, R. R. (1986b). Personality stability and its implications for clinical psychology. *Clinical Psychology Review, 6*, 407–423.

Costa, P. T., Jr., & McCrae, R. R. (1988). Personality in adulthood: A six-year longitudinal study of self-reports and spouse ratings on the NEO Personality Inventory. *Journal of Personality and Social Psychology, 54*, 853–863.

Costa, P. T., Jr., & McCrae, R. R. (1989). *The NEO-PI/NEO-FFI manual supplement.* Odessa, FL: Psychological Assessment Resources, Inc.

Costa, P. T., Jr., McCrae, R. R., & Arenberg, D. (1980). Enduring dispositions in adult males. *Journal of Personality and Social Psychology, 38*, 793–800.

Costa, P. T., Jr., McCrae, R. R., & Arenberg, D. (1983). Recent longitudinal research on personality and aging. In K. W. Schaie (Ed.), *Longitudinal studies of adult psychological development* (pp. 222–265). New York: Guilford Press.

Costa, P. T., Jr., McCrae, R. R., Zonderman, A. B., Barbano, H. E., Lebowitz, B., & Larson, D. M. (1986). Cross-sectional studies of personality in a national sample: 2. Stability in neuroticism, extraversion, and openness. *Psychology and Aging, 1*, 144–149.

Costa, P. T., Jr., Zonderman, A. B., McCrae, R. R., Coroni-Huntley, J., Locke, B. Z., & Barbano, H. E. (1987). Longitudinal analyses of psychological well-being in a national sample: Stability of mean levels. *Journal of Gerontology, 42*, 50–55.

Cumming, E., & Henry, W. (1961). *Growing old.* New York: Basic Books.

Digman, J. M., & Inouye, J. (1986). Further specification of the five robust factors of personality. *Journal of Personality and Social Psychology, 50*, 116–123.

Douglas, K., & Arenberg, D. (1978). Age changes, cohort differences, and cultural change on the Guilford-Zimmerman Temperament Survey. *Journal of Gerontology, 33*, 737–747.

Eichorn, D. H., Clausen, J. A., Haan, N., Honzik, M. P., & Mussen, P. H. (Eds.). (1981). *Present and past in middle life.* New York: Acadmic Press.

Elder, G. H., Jr., & Clipp, E. C. (1988). Combat experience, comradeship, and psychological health. In J. Wilson, Z. Harel, & B. Kahana (Eds.), *Human adaptations to extreme stress: From the Holocaust to Vietnam.* New York: Plenum Press.

Elder, G. H., Jr., Liker, J. K., & Jaworski, B. J. (1984). Hardship in lives: Depression influences from the 1930s to old age in postwar America. In K. McCluskey & H. W. Reese (Eds.), *Life-span developmental psychology: Historical and generational effects* (pp. 161–201). New York: Academic Press.

Erikson, E. H. (1950). *Childhood and society.* New York: Norton.

Farrell, M. P., & Rosenberg, S. D. (1981). *Men at midlife.* Boston: Auburn House.

Finn, S. E. (1986). Stability of personality self-ratings over 30 years: Evidence for an age/cohort interaction. *Journal of Personality and Social Psychology, 50*, 813–818.

Gergen, K. J. (1977). Stability, change, and chance in understanding human development. In N. Datan & H. W. Reese (Eds.), *Life-span developmental psychology: Dialectical perspectives on experimental research* (pp. 135–158). New York: Academic Press.

Gold, D., Andres, D., & Schwartzman, A. (1987). Self-perception of personality at midlife in elderly people: Continuity and change. *Experimental Aging Research, 13*, 197–202.

Gould, R. L. (1978). *Transformations*. New York: Simon and Schuster.

Gutmann, D. L. (1970). Female ego styles and generational conflict. In J. M. Bardwich, E. Douvan, M. S. Horner, & D. L. Gutmann (Eds.), *Feminine personality and conflict* (pp. 77–96). Belmont, CA: Brooks/Cole.

Haan, N., Millsap, R., & Hartka, E. (1986). As time goes by: Change and stability in personality over fifty years. *Psychology and Aging, 1*, 220–232.

Helson, R., & Moane, G. (1987). Personality change in women from college to midlife. *Journal of Personality and Social Psychology, 53*, 176–186.

Hogan, R. T. (1983). Socioanalytic theory of personality. In M. M. Page (Ed.), *1982 Nebraska Symposium on Motivation: Personality—current theory and research* (pp. 55–89). Lincoln, NE: University of Nebraska Press.

Hogan, R., DeSoto, C. B., & Solano, C. (1977). Traits, tests, and personality research. *American Psychologist, 32*, 255–264.

Jessor, R. (1983). The stability of change: Psychosocial development from adolescence to young adulthood. In D. Magnusson & V. L. Allen (Eds.), *Human development: An interactional perspective* (pp. 321–341). New York: Academic Press.

John, O. P., Goldberg, L. R., & Angleitner, A. (1984). Better than the alphabet: Taxonomies of personality-descriptive terms in English, Dutch, and German. In H. J. C. Bonarius, G. L. M. van Heck, & N. G. Smid (Eds.), *Personality psychology in Europe: Theoretical and empirical developments* (pp. 83–100). Lisse, Switzerland: Swets & Zeitlinger.

Jung, C. G. (1933). *Modern man in search of a soul* (W. S. Dell & C. F. Baynes, Trans.). New York: Harcourt Brace Jovanovich.

Kelly, E. L. (1955). Consistency of the adult personality. *American Psychologist, 10*, 659–681.

Lazarus, R. S., & DeLongis, A. (1983). Psychological stress and coping in aging. *American Psychologist, 38*, 245–254.

Leon, G. R., Gillum, B., Gillum, R., & Gouze, M. (1979). Personality stability and chnage over a 30 year period—middle age to old age. *Journal of Consulting and Clinical Psychology, 47*, 517–524.

Levinson, D. J., Darrow, C. N., Klein, E. B., Levinson, M. L., & McKee, B. (1978). *The seasons of a man's life*. New York: Knopf.

Little, B. R. (1983). Personal projects: A rationale and method for investigation. *Environment and Behavior, 15*, 273–309.

Lowenthal, M. F., Thurner, M., & Chiriboga, D. (1975). *Four stages of life*. San Francisco: Jossey-Bass.

Maas, H. S., & Kuypers, J. A. (1974). *From thirty to seventy*. San Francisco: Jossey-Bass.

Maddox, G. L. (1963). Activity and morale: A longitudinal study of selected elderly subjects. *Social Forces, 42*, 195–204.

McAdams, D. P. (1988). Biography, narrative, and lives: An introduction. *Journal of Personality, 56*, 1–18.

McAdams, D. P., & Ochberg, R. L. (Eds.). (1988). Psychobiography and life narratives [Special issue]. *Journal of Personality, 56*(1).

McCrae, R. R. (1982a). Age differences in the use of coping mechanisms. *Journal of Gerontology, 37*, 454–460.

McCrae, R. R. (1982b). Consensual validation of personality traits: Evidence from self-reports and ratings. *Journal of Personality and Social Psychology, 43*, 293–303.

McCrae, R. R., & Costa, P. T., Jr. (1980). Openness to experience and ego level in Loevinger's sentence completion test: Dispositional contributions to developmental models of personality. *Journal of Personality and Social Psychology, 39*, 1179–1190.

McCrae, R. R., & Costa, P. T., Jr. (1982). Self-concept and the stability of personality: Cross-sectional comparisons of self-reports and ratings. *Journal of Personality and Social Psychology, 43*, 1282–1292.

McCrae, R. R., & Costa, P. T., Jr. (1985a). Openness to experience. In R. Hogan & W. H. Jones (Eds.), *Perspectives in personality* (Vol. 1, pp. 145–172). Greenwich, CT: JAI Press.

McCrae, R. R., & Costa, P. T., Jr. (1985b). Updating Norman's "adequate taxonomy": Intelligence and personality dimensions in natural language and in questionnaires. *Journal of Personality and Social Psychology, 49*, 710–721.

McCrae, R. R., & Costa, P. T., Jr. (1987). Validation of the five-factor model of personality across instruments and observers. *Journal of Personality and Social Psychology, 52*, 81–90.

McCrae, R. R., & Costa, P. T., Jr. (1988). Age, personality, and the spontaneous self-concept. *Journal of Gerontology: Social Sciences, 43*, S177–S185.

McCrae, R. R., Costa, P. T., Jr., & Arenberg, D. (1980). Constancy of adult personality structure in adult males: Longitudinal, cross-sectional and times of measurement analyses. *Journal of Gerontology, 35*, 877–883.

Morris, W. (Ed.). (1976). *The American heritage dictionary of the English language.* Boston: Houghton Mifflin.

Mortimer, J. T., Finch, M. D., & Kumka, D. (1982). Persistence and change in development: The multidimensional self-concept. In P. B. Baltes & O. G. Brim, Jr. (Eds.), *Life-span development and behavior* (Vol. 4, pp. 264–315). New York: Academic Press.

Neugarten, B. L. (1964). *Personality in middle and late life.* New York: Atherton Press.

Neugarten, B. L. (Ed.). (1968). *Middle age and aging: A reader in social psychology.* Chicago: University of Chicago Press.

Neugarten, B. L. (1977). Personality and aging. In J. E. Birren & K. W. Schaie (Eds.), *Handbook of the psychology of aging* (1st. ed., pp. 626–649). New York: Van Nostrand Reinhold.

Norman, W. T. (1963). Toward an adequate taxonomy of personality attributes: Replicated factor structure in peer nomination personality ratings. *Journal. of Abnormal and Social Psychology, 66*, 574–583.

Palmore, E. (Ed.). (1970). *Normal aging: Reports from the Duke Longitudinal Study, 1955–1969.* Durham, NC: Duke University Press.

Palmore, E. (Ed.). (1974). *Normal aging II: Reports from the Duke Longitudinal Study, 1970–1973.* Durham, NC: Duke University Press.

Pfeiffer, E. (1977). Psychopathology and social pathology. In J. E. Birren & K. W. Schaie (Eds.), *Handbook of the psychology of aging* (1st ed., pp. 650–671). New York: Van Nostrand Reinhold.

Reichard, S., Livson, F., & Peterson, P. G. (1962). *Aging and personality.* New York: Wiley.

Rosenberg, M. (1979). *Conceiving the self.* New York: Basic Books.

Ross, M., & Conway, M. (1986). Remembering one's own past: The construction of personal histories. In R. M. Sorrentino & E. T. Higgins (Eds.), *Handbook of motivation and cognition: Foundations of social behavior* (pp. 122–144). New York: Guilford Press.

Runyan, W. McK. (1980). A stage-state analysis of the life course. *Journal of Personality and Social Psychology, 38,* 951–962.

Runyan, W. M. (1981). Why did Van Gogh cut off his ear? The problem of alternative explanations in psychobiography. *Journal of Personality and Social Psychology, 40,* 1070–1077.

Ryff, C. D. (1982). Self-perceived personality change in adulthood and aging. *Journal of Personality and Social Psychology, 42,* 108–115.

Ryff, C. D., & Heincke, S. G. (1983). Subjective organization of personality in adulthood and aging. *Journal of Personality and Social Psychology, 44,* 807–816.

Schaie, K. W. (1977). Quasi-experimental research designs in the psychology of aging. In J. E. Birren & K. W. Schaie (Eds.), *Handbook of the psychology of aging* (1st ed., pp. 39–69). New York: Van Nostrand Reinhold.

Schuerger, J. M., Tait, E., & Tavernelli, M. (1982). Temporal stability of personality by questionnaire. *Journal of Personality and Social Psychology, 43,* 176–182.

Shanan, J. (1985). *Personality types and culture in later adulthood.* Basel, Switzerland: Karger.

Sheehy, G. (1976). *Passages: Predictable crises of adult life.* New York: Dutton.

Shock, N. W., Greulich, R. C., Andres, R., Arenberg, D., Costa, P. T., Jr., Lakatta, E. G., & Tobin, J. D. (1984). *Normal human aging: The Baltimore Longitudinal Study of Aging* (NIH Publication No. 84-2450). Bethesda, MD: National Institutes of Health.

Shrauger, J. S., & Osberg, T. M. (1981). The relative accuracy of self-predictions and judgments by others in psychological assessment. *Psychological Bulletin, 90,* 322–351.

Siegler, I. C., George, L. K., & Okun, M. A. (1979). Cross-sequential analysis of adult personality. *Developmental Psychology, 15,* 350–351.

Skolnick, A. (1966). Stability and interrelationships of thematic test imagery over twenty years. *Child Development, 37,* 389–396.

Stevens, D. P., & Truss, C. V. (1985). Stability and change in adult personality over 12 and 20 years. *Developmental Psychology, 21,* 568–584.

Thomae, H. (Ed.). (1976). *Patterns of aging: Findings from the Bonn Longitudinal Study of Aging.* Basel, Switzerland: Karger.

Tupes, E. C., & Christal, R. E. (1961). *Recurrent personality factors based on trait ratings* (USAF ASD Tech. Rep. No. 61-97). Lackland Air Force Base, TX: U. S. Air Force.

Vaillant, G. E. (1977). *Adaptation to life*. Boston: Little, Brown.

Vaillant, G. E., & Drake, R. E. (1985). Maturity of ego defenses in relation to *DSM-III* Axis II personality disorder. *Archives of General Psychiatry, 42*, 597–601.

Vaillant, G. E., & McCullough, L. (1987). The Washington University Sentence Completion Test compared with other measures of adult ego development. *American Journal of Psychiatry, 144*, 1189–1194.

Vaillant, G. E., Bond, M., & Vaillant, C. O. (1986). An empirically validated hierarchy of defense mechanisms. *Archives of General Psychiatry, 43*, 786–794.

VandenBos, G. R. (Ed.). (1986). Psychotherapy research [Special issue]. *American Psychologist, 41*(2).

Whitbourne, S. K., & Waterman, A. S. (1979). Psychosocial development during the adult years: Age and cohort comparisons. *Developmental Psychology, 15*, 373–378.

White, R. W. (Ed.). (1964). *The study of lives: Essays on personality in honor of Henry A. Murray*. New York: Atherton.

Winter, D. G., & Carlson, L. A. (1988). Using motive scores in the psychobiographical study of an individual: The case of Richard Nixon. *Journal of Personality, 56*, 75–104.

Woodruff, D. S., & Birren, J. E. (1972). Age changes and cohort differences in personality. *Developmental Psychology, 6*, 252–259.

MARGARET GATZ

CLINICAL PSYCHOLOGY AND AGING

Margaret Gatz received her BA from Southwestern-at-Memphis, which resolved its identity crisis but contributed to hers by changing its name to Rhodes College. She earned her PhD in clinical psychology in 1972 from Duke University. After a postdoctoral appointment at Duke's Center for the Study of Aging and Human Development, she taught on the faculty of the clinical–community program at University of Maryland until 1979. She then moved to the University of Southern California (USC) to accept the challenge of coordinating the clinical-aging track in USC's Department of Psychology. She remains at USC, where she now serves as professor of psychology, Director of Clinical Training, Senior Research Associate at the Ethel Percy Andrus Gerontology Center, and Faculty Athletics Representative.

Gatz is a Fellow of the American Psychological Association (APA) and of the Gerontological Society of America. Within APA, she is a member of the Committee on Accreditation. In Division 20 (Adult Development and Aging) she has been newsletter editor and chair of the convention program committee and is now the council representative.

Gatz's research interests encompass a variety of topics related primarily to mental health and aging. Current funded projects, carried out in collaboration with colleagues ranging geographically from Stockholm to South Pasadena, include an examination of the decision to use electroconvulsive therapy in the treatment of older adults, a longitudinal study of three-generational families, and an investigation of dementia in twins. She has an abiding interest in sense of personal control and autonomy and a recurring impulse to scrutinize well-known assumptions that have little empirical basis.

USC's Graduate Association of Students in Psychology (GASP) has recognized Gatz for Outstanding Performance as a Mentor in 1985 and for Outstanding Performance as a Graduate Course Instructor in 1987 for her teaching of intervention with older adults.

CLINICAL PSYCHOLOGY AND AGING

The purpose of this chapter is to introduce the psychologist to essential issues in clinical work with older adults. There are two major parts. In Part 1, I develop case examples with older adult clients in order to illustrate the nature of the clinical problems presented and the application of empirical and conceptual literature on aging to working clinically with this population.

In Part 2, I reflect on the field of clinical psychology and aging. Ten years ago there was a master lecture series on adult development and aging, at which Lawton talked on "clinical geropsychology" (Lawton, 1978). Therefore, I specifically consider changes that have taken place over the last decade, concluding with several prophecies about the next decade. In 10 years the next master lecturer on clinical psychology and aging will have a place from which to start.

PART 1: ELEMENTS IN WORKING CLINICALLY WITH OLDER ADULTS

In this section, I mix clinical case examples with theoretical points and references to empirical literature. There is more emphasis on understanding the person and the problem and relatively less emphasis on techniques. This emphasis results from a sincere conviction that a good understanding is the most important contribution a clinician makes to any solution. This section could be called a casebook, as the format was in part inspired by Neale, Oltmanns, and Davison's (1982) *Case Studies in Abnormal Psychology*.

Preface

The casebook has a preface, in which the author imagines being asked two questions: What can possibly be interesting about working with older clients? And, what theoretical perspective do you take?

The Challenge of the Aged Client

What is interesting about older clients? Actually, the very complexity of the cases is part of the fascination. The casebook describes some of the less complicated cases in order to illustrate the main types of problems, but the hallmark of clinical practice with older adults is the necessity to begin with differential diagnosis, followed by the answer that more than one factor is most likely contributing to the problem. For example, as shown by Reifler's work (Teri & Reifler, 1987), clients are depressed *and* demented, not simply depressed *or* demented.

The clinician working with elderly patients must almost always consider not only the aging client but also the family (cf. Herr & Weakland, 1979; Smyer, 1987). Here, the word *family* should be taken to denote (a) multiple generations, particularly elderly parents and their adult children, as well as (b) informal social networks who are not kin by blood or marriage, especially cases in which the older person was never married or was childless. There are often situations that can be conceptualized both as the problem of an older adult and as a family systems problem. Central to such family cases is the clinical question, Who is the client? At least three subquestions arise: Who is identified as having a problem? Who says this person has a problem? Who comes to the clinic? The complexity is marvelous.

Another aspect that makes working with older adults interesting and rewarding is that often these are individuals or families who have been very ordinary or normal their entire lives and now are faced with an extraordinary, abnormal situation. In short, although clinical psychol-

Preparation of this chapter was facilitated by a grant from the Robert Ellis Simon Foundation. The author thanks Irene Takaragawa for her bibliographic and administrative assistance.

ogists cannot cure dementia, these are people who can be helped. Finally, as Felton (1982) noted, given the vast neglect, "[i]t is difficult *not* to feel moved to act to increase the quantity and quality of care available to older persons" (p. 23).

Theoretical Framework

Now the second question: What theoretical perspective do you take? A therapist needs two things, a model of person and a model of change. Each of these models has developmental features; beyond that, it seems possible to bring a variety of psychotherapeutic theories and techniques, according to one's own preference.

Model of person means both a generic model of people and a specific set of hypotheses about the individual client. My generic model of person draws on life span developmental theory, as expressed by scholars such as Baltes (Baltes & Danish, 1980), Schaie (1988), and Riegel (1976). A life span perspective provides the psychologist with a way of thinking about aging in the context of the entire life and of the events that influence that life (Smyer, 1987). Several points are often made by these theorists.

The first is interindividual variability: There is a great diversity among older adults, such that on any given attribute (from intelligence to income), the distribution of scores for older adults will overlap to some extent the distribution of scores for younger adults (Schaie, 1988). As Smyer (1987) explained, the best pedictor of how people will be when they are old is how they were when they were younger.

The second point is to distinguish theoretically between age and cohort. Here, *cohort* refers to the generation into which the person was born and all of the broad social and cultural influences that accompany growing up and growing older in a particular time in history. Thus, in a given individual's life, age is inseparable from cohort. Trying to be sensitive to cohort myself, I often adopt the phrase "individuals now old" to refer to the current cohort of older adults.

A third concept to be included in a life span perspective is multiple interaction (i.e., appreciation of the interrelations among social, biological, and psychological aspects of development). It is frequently pointed out that these issues may have greater interactive consequences with advancing age (Eisdorfer, 1987; Smyer, 1987).

A fourth point in a life span developmental model is that the individual is not simply the passive recipient of events and changes. The individual is an actor in his or her own life, coping and managing the various changes, creating other changes, and creating meaning (Piaget, cited in Flavell, 1963; Riegel, 1976; Smith, 1968). The spiral of interactions between external influences, primarily the demands of social reality, and the active individual is the basis for descriptions of the life cycle, such as the theories of Erikson (1963) or Levinson (1978).

Possibly my favorite writer on psychopathology is Shapiro, author of *Neurotic Styles* (1965) and more recently *Autonomy and Rigid Character* (1981). Shapiro does not write about aging at all, but he uses developmental theory (both psychodynamic and cognitive) to understand the differences in adaptation that describe various pathologies. Pathology is defined by distortions in processes of constructing the view of the world to which one then reacts.

The *model of change* also draws on a developmental perspective. According to this view, psychotherapeutic change is a subset of human development, and the same processes are applicable to remediation or psychotherapy as to preventive interventions. Developmental change is achieved through processes of disequilibrium and then reordering (Riegel, 1976). Writers who have been interested in mechanisms of change that bridge diverse schools are especially pertinent (e.g., Mahoney's [1981] master lecture on psychotherapy and human change processes, Pavey's work on mechanisms of change, and Watzlawick, Weakland, and Fisch's book [1974] called *Change*). Implicit in this viewpoint is the embeddedness of change within one's understanding of the problem and the person.

Four mechanisms of change emerge from an integration of psychotherapy research with life span developmental theory (Gatz, Popkin, Pino, & VandenBos, 1985): self-efficacy, therapeutic relationship, meaning, and learning. Although conceptually each has earned mention, as will become evident, they may frequently overlap in application.

Self-efficacy encompasses sense of control or mastery, autonomy, positive expectancies, hope, morale, and self-esteem. This interrelated set of variables is cited as important in virtually all psychological interventions, sometimes as part of the aspects of therapy called "nonspecifics," at other times as a deliberate focus. It is the phenomenology of these concepts that is crucial to emphasize; for example, Sarton (1973), in her work of fiction *As We Are Now*, offers a poignant description of the fragility of the person who is old and dependent. In general, it is suggested that the process of helping is more effective to the extent that help can be delivered in a way that makes the recipient feel self-esteem and control (Karuza, Rabinowitz, & Zevon, 1986; Rodin, 1980). Examples of techniques for increasing sense of efficacy include giving older adults options so that they can make choices (Rodin, 1980) or using a psychoeducational approach to provide information to older adults in order to permit greater competence and control over the environment (Slivinske & Fitch, 1987).

Therapeutic relationship includes all of the ways in which the therapist functions to make the client feel understood and to provide necessary external social reality, ranging from demonstrating caring and empathy, to giving information, to providing a sounding board for problem solving, to being the catalyst for the client's reconstructing his or her view of the interpersonal world. In *As We Are Now*, Sarton (1973) stated that true caring shows itself by the quality of listening.

Meaning is intended to span both the term as used by Mahoney (1981) to describe reintegrations following disequilibria as well as the wider sense of achieving an integration of one's life experiences in older adulthood and coming to terms with the life one has lived (cf. Erikson's [1963] concept of ego integrity as the eighth stage of human development or Tobin's [1986] notion of reaffirming the self and confronting one's finitude [Lieberman & Tobin, 1983]). The idea of life review, or the constructive use of reminiscence, and through this process restoring ego integrity, has long been a part of the literature on psychological interventions with older adults (Lewis & Butler, 1974; Sherman, 1987).

Learning encompasses behavior therapy as well as educative activities that provide information to clients or groups. Learning and memory processes have, of course, been a focus of much research in normal adult development and aging. Implied by this mechanism is application of what has been learned from that body of research to methods of teaching interpersonal skills, coping mechanisms, and so on.

The Casebook

There are three sections to this "casebook"[1]—Depression, Dementia, and A Character—in which six cases are presented. The coverage is illustrative, not comprehensive. The choices reflect the fact that depression and dementia are the most common mental disorders among older adults (for an excellent review, see LaRue, Dessonville, & Jarvik, 1985). Other conditions—which cannot be encompassed in the space of this chapter— are also seen, such as simple paranoid psychosis, late schizophrenia (sometimes called paraphrenia), delirium, alcohol abuse, and anxiety (Goldstrom et al., 1987; LaRue et al., 1985; Post, 1987).

Depression

The case. Sarah Feldon phoned the clinic at the suggestion of a clinical psychologist in Seattle, Dr. Patrick Wells. Mrs. Feldon was in Seattle visiting her daughter, Marsha, a special education teacher. Mrs. Feldon shared with Marsha some of her feelings of unhappiness. In fact, she probably could not entirely hide them. Marsha apparently was seeing

---

[1] The author gratefully acknowledges the contributions of Steve Zarit, who founded the Andrus Older Adult Center; Cynthia Pearson, who has team taught the graduate practicum for several years; and the students who served as the therapists. The cases are real but names and details about clients are disguised, and some case examples are amalgams of several similar clinic cases. The clients are not very different from those that one would see at any clinic with an interest in serving aged persons.

Patrick Wells for therapy, and she took her mother to see Wells for a consultation. Wells told Mrs. Feldon that she had a major clinical depression and that she should seek therapy once she got back home. He contacted the university medical center for referrals, and they were familiar with our clinic. Mrs. Feldon followed through as soon as she returned home, and an intake was scheduled.

Mrs. Feldon, at age 76, was an attactive, well-dressed, and nicely coiffed woman who appeared younger than her age. She was intelligent, well read, and articulate. For the past year, Mrs. Feldon reported, she had been feeling unhappy. It began as moodiness and at various times included feelings of worthlessness and low self-esteem, loss of energy, insomnia, forgetfulness, difficulty in concentrating, some crying spells, occasional periods of panic, and even thoughts of suicide.

Mrs. Feldon had been widowed for 12 years. Both of her parents were also deceased, she had a sister in Pennsylvania, and she had a son in Michigan as well as her daughter. Neither child was married. Mrs. Feldon described herself as severely depressed following her husband's death, although she managed to pull herself out of it. She could think of a few other times in her life that she had felt unhappy, but nothing so protracted or profound as what she was now feeling.

Three months earlier Mrs. Feldon's aunt died. Mrs. Feldon had been very close to her aunt for most of her life. The aunt had a home in Carmel, California, and operated an art studio. This aunt was an unusual woman. The younger sister of Mrs. Feldon's mother, she had run off to San Francisco as a young woman, had an illegitimate daughter while living with a writer, and had continued to live a bohemian life-style. Mrs. Feldon paid frequent long visits to her aunt, particularly in the years following her husband's death, assisting with the studio as her aunt grew older and becoming friendly with the circle of artists who frequented the studio. The aunt's own daughter—an only child—had died childless; the daughter's husband (the aunt's son-in-law) rarely visited even when the daughter was alive. He lived in New York City, where he worked as an accountant. The aunt regarded him as hopelessly conventional.

Mrs. Feldon had always felt that her aunt was more sympathetic than her own mother because the aunt supported her politics, her interest in literature, and so forth. She thought of her aunt and her aunt's friends in Carmel as her real social life. She even had a bit of a flirtation with one of the men, a widower named Leonard. He was the only man in whom she had taken a serious interest since her husband's death. Just after her aunt's death, Leonard was found to have cancer that required a colostomy. At his own daughter's insistence, he moved in with her in Chico, in northern California. He felt that he could not explain to his daughter about Sarah, and contact became awkward. In contrast to Carmel, in Los Angeles Mrs. Feldon's acquaintaince all seemed to be old and frail, even though they were not actually any older than she was, and all of them were women. Mrs. Feldon referred to them as the "withering widows."

The aunt died suddenly of a heart attack. Although the aunt was in her 90s, her death was a surprise. Another surprise was that Mrs. Feldon was not included in her aunt's will, although she had expected to receive something from the estate. Instead, the money all went to the son-in-law and to a new Carmel city park. The money would have been helpful; Mrs. Feldon was at that time very concerned about her finances. The symbolic meaning of her aunt's action was also troublesome because it seemed to belie the closeness Mrs. Feldon had felt. In addition, because of the situation, Mrs. Feldon felt uncomfortable returning to Carmel. Thus, she also was stripped of her best friends. She explained that she suddenly felt old, which she had not felt previously. Moreover, of course, she felt that she could not discuss any of this with the "withering widows."

The therapist doing the intake used a checklist of *DSM-III* (American Psychiatric Association, 1980) criteria for major depressive disorder. Mrs. Feldon easily qualified. She was not judged a risk for suicide at that time. Mrs. Feldon was given the Center for Epidemiological Studies Depression Scale (CES–D; Radloff, 1977) to complete, on which she scored 34, well above the clinical cutoff. The therapist also administered the Mini-Mental State Examination (MMSE; Folstein, Folstein, & McHugh, 1975), on which Mrs. Feldon scored 28 of 30 correct, confirming the impression of intact cognitive status.

Mrs. Feldon had been taking sleeping pills prescribed by her physician when she reported her insomnia to him, as well as medications for high blood pressure and for hypothyroid functioning.

Conceptualization and treatment. Psychological disorders of older adults can be roughly divided along three axes: organic brain disorders (or dementing conditions); lifelong characteristics, including functional disorders; and late-life stress or special issues of later life (Gatz et al., 1985). These are illustrated in Figure 1. Sarah Feldon's depression was viewed by both herself and her therapist as a later-life disorder. Sarah was someone whose lifelong functioning had not been disturbed but whose psychological difficulties arose in late life.

Mrs. Feldon had had periods of depression before, but it was not evident that they would meet diagnostic criteria for major depressive disorder, and she had been able to cope without assistance. Although she regarded herself as having been a somewhat unusual person all of her life, this had never before been a source of difficulty. As the case details make evident, aging and the way in which her life developed conspired to make this time so uniquely stressful.

Various writers have discussed how depression manifests itself in aged persons. Many have expressed concern that depression not be overlooked in older adults. For instance, it would be a mistake to tell Mrs. Feldon that her feelings were just something to expect at her age. On the other hand, existential struggles or sadness after losses should not be overdiagnosed (Kermis, 1986; LaRue et al., 1985). Perhaps, not surprisingly, Blazer, Hughes, and George (1987) have described findings from

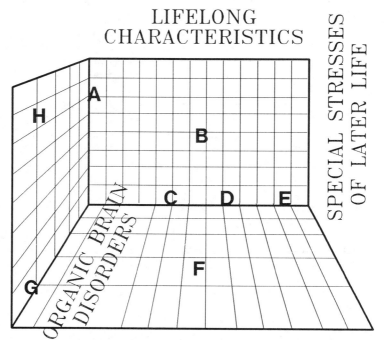

Figure 1. Three-dimensional classification of psychological problems of older adults. Examples indicate how typical disorders might locate on the three axes: A = grief reaction after the illness or death of a spouse; B = narcissistic personality reaction to severe limitations due to poor physical health; C = personality disorder; D = endogenous depression; E = schizophrenia spectrum disorder/paraphrenia; F = dependent personality with cognitive decline due to stroke/multi-infarcts; G = Alzheimer's disease; and H = delirium induced by poor nutrition and iatrogenic drug effects

Epidemiologic Catchment Area data showing a low prevalence of major depressive disorder in older adults but substantial levels of depressed mood and dysphoria.

Among the treatments that have been used for depression in older adults are behavioral therapy, cognitive therapy, brief psychodynamic approaches, and supportive approaches (Gutmann, Griffin, & Grunes, 1982; Nemiroff & Colarusso, 1985; Newton, Brauer, Gutmann, & Grunes, 1986; Thompson, Gallagher, & Breckenridge, 1987). In a variation of cognitive therapy, Scogin, Hamblin, and Beutler (1987) used bibliotherapy in which the book *Feeling Good* (Burns, 1981) was read at home and discussed. Research results from Gallagher and Thompson (1981; Thompson, Davies, Gallagher, & Krantz, 1986) have shown that cognitive and behavioral treatments were more effective with depressed individuals without endogenous features.

Mrs. Feldon agreed to 8 months of weekly sessions. The therapist used some behavioral techniques, focusing on monitoring mood, pleasant and unpleasant activities in relation to mood, and trying to encourage her to increase her activity level. Relaxation training also was instituted (Zeiss & Lewinsohn, 1986). The therapist then assigned *Feeling Good* for her to read. They talked a lot about why this particular time in Mrs. Feldon's life had been so difficult and how to try to prevent such episodes from escalating into severe depression in the future. Without engaging in extensive life review, the therapist encouraged Mrs. Feldon to put this episode in the context of her whole life. Mrs. Feldon still called her friends the "withering widows," but she started engaging in more activities in Los Angeles.

Mrs. Feldon also saw the clinic's consulting psychiatrist, who prescribed Xanax to control the panic and help with the insomnia, and he spoke to her physician about her blood pressure medication. Many blood pressure medications have depressive side effects. The physician changed Mrs. Feldon from Enduronyl to Dydzideil, a blood pressure medication that was known to have fewer depressive side effects.

After several months Mrs. Feldon, on her own initiative, reduced her use of Xanax and had no difficulties in terms of mood or sleep. After about 6 months, Mrs. Feldon called in to cancel a session. She had to fly East to be with her sister, who had suffered a stroke. When Mrs. Feldon came in for her next session 2 weeks later, the therapist expected something of a setback. Mrs. Feldon admitted that she had been depressed and had used Xanax again, but she seemed able to apply what she had learned about depression to pull herself back together. She explained to the therapist that her sister's health problems were very difficult for her but that "sad is different from the crazy grief when you're depressed."

Six months after terminating therapy, Mrs. Feldon completed another CES–D, on which she scored 6 (i.e., not depressed).

Contrasting case. Mrs. Lois Kinder came in with her son, Al, who had phoned and made an appointment for his mother. Mrs. Kinder, aged 66, was very depressed. Her CES–D was 32, and her MMSE score (a standard part of the intake interview procedure) was 25. The son felt that his father was not helpful to his mother. He described his mother's history of depression going back at least 30 years when Mr. Kinder had an affair with another woman. At that time, Mrs. Kinder had electroconvulsive therapy (ECT). She had ECT again 8 years ago, when she stopped working because of her husband's insistence that a woman's place was in the home, and 3 years ago, when her husband had serious complications following surgery. In between she had multiple hospitalizations, without ECT, and trials of various antidepressants. At the time of her visit to the clinic her physician had her on Valium. Mrs. Kinder expressed feelings of hopelessness, stating that "nothing can possibly help me now." She also complained of stomach pains. Al wanted his mother to get off medications and talk to someone about her problems.

In brief, Mrs. Kinder presented a case of lifelong depression that contrasts markedly to that of Mrs. Feldon.

Dementia

The case. Rudy Martinez and his wife, Aurora, both aged 70, contacted the clinic initially because of a newspaper announcement concerning people with memory problems and their family caregivers. Rudy phoned to describe Aurora's problems and to request an evaluation. Rudy said that Aurora was losing her memory, misplacing things, and denying she had put them there when Rudy found them. Aurora made it very difficult for Rudy to help her, alternately withdrawing completely or becoming extremely critical of him. He felt that her personality had changed.

At the clinic, the Martinezes provided more social history. Forty years ago they moved to Santa Torino, a small city east of Los Angeles. Mr. Martinez was the son of immigrants, who moved to California when he was a youngster. His parents encouraged him to stay in school and get as much education as he could. He worked as a probation officer until age 62, when he retired. He has continued to do various odd jobs around the Santa Torino courthouse—such as overseeing jurors' parking—for token pay. Mrs. Martinez, in contrast to her husband, claimed that her ancestors helped to settle California. She worked as the administrative assistant for a small community agency that assists youth in finding jobs. She retired about 5 years ago, having earlier reduced to part-time work, and was still continuing to volunteer whenever her help was needed. Twenty years earlier, Mrs. Martinez had been elected to the Santa Torino City Council, the first minority member in that city's history. Mr. Martinez dated Aurora's problems to the last reelection campaign, which she lost, 3 years ago. He felt that her memory was slipping, and it showed when she talked to voters. Nor would she let him help with the campaign, as he had in previous elections.

Mrs. Martinez complained that her husband had no confidence in her abilities and was treating her like a child. Mr. Martinez was frustrated by his wife. He felt she could not make plans anymore, so she blocked his. He also felt that perhaps he could not continue his occasional work at the courthouse anymore because of her needs. Rudy wanted to sell their house—all 4 children were grown and gone—and move into a smaller place. She did not seem able to do housework. He could not take care of the place without assistance, and they could not afford help.

Mr. Martinez had recently discovered that he had elevated cholesterol and was strongly advised to control his diet. He was following this advice poorly, however, and was overweight.

At the intake interview, Mrs. Martinez scored 24 of 30 correct on the MMSE. She did not know the date. She could not perform serial 7s or do a delayed recall task. She wrung her hands and spoke in a very low voice.

When both were present, she let Rudy speak for her unless he was asked not to. When Aurora was seen alone, she described her husband as becoming upset and screaming at her whenever she forgot anything or did anything wrong. Tears came to her eyes as she talked. There were a number of discrepancies. For example, Rudy said that Aurora's sleep was very poor, that she got up and paced. Aurora said that her sleep was fine.

During their entire marriage, the Martinezes reported that they seldom confided in one another. Both were socially committed to the education of their own children and to the betterment of Latinos. They shared ideals but little warmth or affection. Neither of them had close friends.

Mrs. Martinez was scheduled for neuropsychological assessment. Both of them were given some personality and behavioral assessment forms to complete, in part because Rudy felt that Aurora would be more likely to cooperate if he were being evaluated, too. Mr. Martinez's depression was elevated on the MMPI, and on a marital adjustment scale he reported being unhappy in the marital relationship. In general, he downplayed problems and endorsed the belief that they could be solved by effort. Rudy commented several times that he hoped the clinic would discover that Aurora was just faking it, that she did not really have a problem.

Mrs. Martinez's chief complaint was Mr. Martinez. She felt that he was trying to destroy the family. On cognitive testing, she gave slow responses and vague answers; the only spontaneous conversation concerned their children and their careers. She made numerous requests for repetition of test instructions. She gave conflicting historical information, for example, at one time saying that Rudy had retired 5 years ago, at another time saying that it had been 14 years. On the Wechsler Adult Intelligence Scale–Revised (WAIS–R), her Verbal, Performance, and Full Scale IQs were 94, 78, and 86, respectively. She was unable to do the Block Design subtest, lining the blocks up in a row rather than keeping them within the square format. She did not seem distressed by poor performance except on memory items, on which she became upset and refused to continue. On verbal fluency, she was slightly impaired. Copying figures was slow but adequate, but she could not draw a clock without a model to copy. On measures of marital adjustment, Aurora described herself as being unhappy, and she saw Rudy as misperceiving her desires.

Medical records from Mrs. Martinez's neurologist were secured. The report referred to a 10-year history of memory complaints, in which the first neurological evaluation was entirely within the normal range, so she was simply reassured. Five years later she returned with similar complaints. A computerized tomography (CT) scan was negative and she was told that the memory problems were "simply old age." At the third evaluation, 2-1/2 years previous to the clinic intake, the neurologist reported memory testing to be fairly normal for her age, although her responses were slow. Verbal fluency was slightly impaired. His impression was "dementia of unknown etiology." The therapist noted that although the neuropsychological testing 2-1/2 years earlier had been minimal, there appeared to have been some decline between the third neurology evaluation and the current testing at the clinic.

Two of the Martinez children—Alex and Suzette—accompanied their mother to the first testing session. The parents proudly introduced their children and requested that the therapist talk with them. There were 4 children altogether: Suzette (aged 42), Melinda (aged 40), Alex (aged 35), and Sally (aged 27). All had graduated from college, and Suzette earned a master's degree. Suzette worked as a research technician at the earthquake research laboratory at California Institute of Technology; the other 3 had careers in business. Melinda resided in Kansas City, and Alex was thinking of moving there, too. Sally was about to get married. She had been closest to the parents in recent years, moving back into the family home after finishing college and only moving out again in the past couple of years. The other 2 siblings said Sally helped out with keeping the family's financial records.

Suzette and Alex considered their father to be a terrible tyrant, suggesting that it was a logical extension of a culturally approved male dominant role but nonetheless oppressive. They described growing up. Their father made no effort to spend time with the family, leaving the responsibilities of the house entirely to their mother. He was very punitive if the children ever made a mistake or did not aspire to high goals. He yelled at their mother and at them. The children felt that their mother's current problems were due to their father's domineering manner, in essence, that he finally drove their mother crazy. According to the others, Sally attributed her mother's memory lapses to "just old age," reminding everyone that this was what the neurologist had told them. The therapist explained the evaluation process to Suzette and Alex and suggested a family meeting in a few weeks to review the results of their parents' assessment.

Conceptualization and treatment. Initially, the most important treatment for this couple was assessment and feedback, such that they had a good understanding of exactly what was going on. A number of hypotheses required evaluation in this case.

The main concern was Mrs. Martinez's memory. To what extent was the apparent decline in cognitive function attributable to a depressive disorder as opposed to cerebral impairment? Conversely, it could have been that there was some depression as a consequence of awareness of cognitive decline or that the decline represented normal age-related change.

Furthermore, to what extent were marital difficulties implicated? Mrs. Martinez and her children placed the blame there. Alternatively, certainly marital stress could have exacerbated memory problems brought on by organic changes.

Additionally, Mr. Martinez seemed depressed but unwilling to admit it, and he showed poor health habits that eventually could jeopardize his ability to help his wife.

Differential diagnosis of depression and dementia is a major topic area in aging and mental disorders (LaRue et al., 1985; Zarit, Orr, & Zarit, 1985). Older patients have been observed to present cognitive deficits that improve when their depression is treated. At one time among gerontological clinicians, it was a rule of thumb that if a patient complained of memory problems, the diagnosis was depression. If a family member complained about a patient's memory, then dementia might be a possibility. However, it has more recently become apparent that in the early stages of dementia, especially in intelligent older adults, the patient may be the first one sensitive to his or her own cognitive changes. In this case, Mrs. Martinez seemed to be the first to notice her own changes.

Dementia is almost exclusively a syndrome of old age. The prevalence of moderate to severe dementias in older adults is typically estimated to be around 5% (LaRue et al., 1985). The most common of the dementias is Alzheimer's disease (accounting for roughly 60% of all cases of dementia), followed by multi-infarct dementia (MID), sometimes referred to as vascular dementia (20%), and a mixture of the two (15%). Although this summary represents the current literature, perhaps it should be noted that these figures are controversial in that vascular dementia may be overdiagnosed (Brust, 1988), whereas the incidence of mixed cases may actually be higher (Alafuzoff, Iqbal, Friden, Adolfsson, & Winblad, 1987). Dementia of the Alzheimer's type (DAT) is a progressive and irreversible condition associated with increasing impairment of cognition and then self-care, with no disturbance of consciousness, and characterized by brain changes of unknown etiology.

Diagnosis of Alzheimer's disease is made by *excluding* other causes of the symptoms. First, potentially reversible processes that may be producing or exacerbating the cognitive symptoms are differentiated and treated, including side effects of drugs, malnutrition, metabolic and endocrine disorders, infectious diseases, and brain tumors (Zarit, Orr, et al., 1985). Second, irreversible but nonprogressive brain damage such as head trauma or strokes are identified and differentiated from progressive disorders. Third, differentiation of Alzheimer's disease from MID or other progressive dementias relies to large extent on history and medical features. For instance, Alzheimer's disease has a gradual onset and steady course of deterioration; MID would be associated with a history of stroke or hypertension.

The best way of diagnosing any dementing illness is to follow the patient over time. Over the course of treating this case, more decline was witnessed. Initially it was easier to be sympathetic to Rudy's wish that this was all deliberate on Aurora's part and to Aurora's complaint that the problem was all in the marriage. Over 2 years of seeing this family,

Mrs. Martinez dropped 20 points on the WAIS–R. Her score on the MMSE was now 12; for example, she could not handle multistage commands. She remained very pleasant socially. Subsequent visits to the neurologist supported a diagnosis of Alzheimer's disease.

This case offers a good example of how an individual's problem becomes a family problem. Families of frail elders have been described as the hidden victims (e.g., Zarit, Orr, et al., 1985), and a number of scholars have documented their psychological distress (Anthony-Bergstone, Zarit, & Gatz, 1988; George & Gwyther, 1986). Following Zarit, Orr, et al. (1985), once the patient was assessed, family intervention included three components: provision of knowledge (information about specific deficits, the disease process, and prognosis); assistance in family problem solving related to the behavioral difficulties caused by the impairments; and social support.

In this case, the therapist devoted special attention to patterns of marital communication. Feeling supported rather than attacked could only help, not worsen, Mrs. Martinez's memory, and she could enhance the likelihood of sympathetic responses from her husband by letting him know when she was having problems rather than blaming him. Teri and Gallagher (in press) have written about carrying out behavioral interventions with moderately to severely demented patients; thus, cognitive impairment need not preclude individual or couples' therapy.

For a variety of reasons, every attempt to schedule a family meeting met with failure, although one or another of the children would sometimes come to the clinic with his or her parents. The children clung to the notion that the whole problem was their father's fault. They reported terrible things that he was continuing to do, such as preparing Mexican TV dinners for himself and Aurora. The therapist was impressed, in contrast to the children, with the extent to which Rudy seemed to have become an attentive caregiver. The therapist did not discount earlier stories, but assumed that Rudy had been able to make some changes. Rudy remained resistant to examining his own psychological issues. The therapist's concern was that eventually Rudy's own health problems might make it impossible for him to continue providing the level of care that he was presently giving and that others might not be available to step in.

Exemplifying gradual termination, Rudy has continued to telephone the clinic from time to time when there has been a change or he needed advice. Most recently, he sought help in locating a dentist who would be able to handle someone with Aurora's cognitive impairments. Whenever he calls, he is encouraged to join a support group. At last contact, he was feeling that things were going all right, that he might soon get the house in shape to put it on the market, and that the children were visiting more frequently so they could get a better appreciation of their mother's condition.

Contrasting case. Wilma Greene, aged 69, called regarding her husband, Chester, who is 72 years old. Chester was diagnosed with Alzheimer's disease 2 years ago. She felt she had no time to get out of the house.

They both came to the clinic for an intake interview. Chester had two strokes, one 10 years ago, the second 2 years after that. At present, he had high blood pressure, for which he was taking medication. He also had glaucoma in both eyes. Wilma reported that recently Chester had become nonresponsive to her when she was talking to him. He would ask questions, the same ones over and over again. He followed her around the house. He had become suspicious of her and would accuse her of having an affair and taking his things. She joked that she did not have time to have an affair, that she was never gone long enough to do anything. She had taken the car away from him because she felt he was not a safe driver.

Mrs. Greene traced the onset to about 4 years ago when Chester became disoriented and confused after a car accident, in which he tried to leave the scene. According to Mrs. Greene, 2 years ago the doctor said that the problem was Alzheimer's disease, on the basis of CT scan and electrocardiographic results.

Mrs. Greene mentioned that *The 36-Hour Day* (Mace & Rabins, 1981) had been helpful to her. She was interested in referrals for adult daycare, as she felt she must get more time for herself or she would become ill and unable to care for Chester. Wilma had a large social network within driving distance, including a son with whom she frequently talked on the phone and several grandchildren whom she saw often.

Chester scored 5 of 10 correct on the Mental Status Questionnaire (Kahn, Goldfarb, Pollack, & Peck, 1960), and 12 of 30 correct on the MMSE. He was clearly impaired. Wilma scored 29 on the Burden Interview (Zarit, Reever, & Bach-Peterson, 1981) and 17 on the CES–D, indicating the stress that she described.

Conceptualization and treatment. The Greenes are an example of an uncomplicated caregiving case. Mrs. Greene came in for individual sessions and a support group. The group was helpful in giving her ideas for solving some of the behavior problems, for giving her suggestions how to let her family help her out more, and for obtaining more referrals for activities for Chester.

A number of writers have been concerned with how a health crisis, such as Alzheimer's disease, affects the family system (Bengtson & Kuypers, 1985; Herr & Weakland, 1979; Pruchno, Blow, & Smyer, 1984). In the Martinez and the Greene families, two different examples are provided.

Bengtson and Kuypers (1985) suggested that a crisis may precipitate a cyclical process of vulnerability, including stereotypic meanings placed by the family on the crisis and inadequacy of coping skills. Both Bengtson and Kuypers (1985) and Sherman (1981) have proposed counseling methods that use inputs into this vicious cycle to reverse it.

In the Sherman (1981) version, there are four phases. In the first phase, services are provided to address the immediate crisis, such as seeing to physical or financial needs. There is greater use of community resources, and the therapist takes an educative or even directive role. In Mrs. Greene's case, referrals to community services that would let her get out of the house represented the immediate need. All clients may not require inputs here.

In the second phase, the therapist provides support, bolstering the client's coping strategies and existing defense mechanisms. For example, Mrs. Greene used humor to cope. The therapeutic approach is supportive and still fits under the rubric of crisis intervention.

In the third phase, the therapist uses various techniques to improve the client's coping and increase sense of control or mastery of the client's life situation. In the Greene case, in this phase the therapist might push Mrs. Greene to discuss level of involvement in caregiving for Chester by other family members and to examine her own expectations of herself, realistic and unrealistic (Bengtson & Kuypers, 1985).

Sherman's fourth phase represents long-term therapeutic goals: altering the client's basic attitudes toward self in order to promote experiencing one's life as meaningful. Interestingly, Sherman redefines life review therapy such that it fits into a cognitive model, including the client's engaging in examination of past values in order to dispute the belief that one's self-worth is defined by one's functional value in society. Not all clients move beyond brief intervention into long-term therapy. In the cases above, Mrs. Feldon did the most work at this phase.

Such a model seemingly offers a useful heuristic for organizing presumptive modifications of psychotherapy with older adults, suggesting which might be applicable to different cases.

Another contrast. Harold Saunders was a 54-year-old man who called because he felt that he was beginning to exhibit symptoms of Alzheimer's disease. During the intake interview, he was extremely nervous. His father was diagnosed with Alzheimer's 3 years ago. His grandmother was senile and institutionalized the last 20 years of her life. Harold described memory problems for 2 years; he said his wife had been concerned for 5 years. The main memory problem was forgetting people's names, including people he had known for over 20 years. For example, he recently had lunch with a person and suddenly could not remember his name. His secretary, who was aware of the problem, had even made it a point to prompt him before he left for the lunch meeting. His wife had told him that he forgets major events, such as places they have just visited together. Recently he got lost when driving. He reported that his father had a similar problem, which he had handled by simply driving around until he found where he was going. Harold also experienced going into a room in his own house and then forgetting why he was there.

Saunders worked in a management position at a movie studio. His life at work was built around meetings, and recently he had begun to forget them. His secretary typically reminded him. According to Harold, his wife was convinced that he was slipping month by month; his secretary allegedly said that he had not changed in 10 years. Because of upheavals in the industry, about 5 years ago Harold's job was threatened. Consequently he began working on a real estate license, so that he would have an alternative source of income. For the present he planned to put all of the proceeds of his real estate activity into a special money market account to be used to defray expenses of his own institutionalization once he had deteriorated enough to need to place himself in a nursing home.

Harold's physician had prescribed medication for his anxiety. Harold wondered whether he should request a CT scan for the memory problems.

On the MMSE Harold had 30 of 30 correct. His performance on an Alzheimer's screening battery—including recall of lists, naming, verbal fluency, and producing a complex drawing from recall—was impeccable. On the CES–D he scored 20, slightly higher than the cutoff that would suggest a clinically significant level of depression.

The impression of the therapist doing the intake was that Mr. Saunders had "alzism." Alzism is the tendency to become excessively aware of one's own memory slips, to become too ready to attribute any problem of an older adult to Alzheimer's disease, or both. Kirby and Harper (1988), referred to a diagnosis of "hysterical pseudodementia" (alzism). In Mr. Saunders's case, his memory complaints seemed to be related to the various stresses he was under, and he was invited to consider therapy for his depression and anxiety.

A Character

Petunia Phillips, aged 68, phoned concerning her depression. About 2 months ago she had called Toni Grant, a local talk radio psychologist. She did not actually get on the air, but the people at the station advised her to get involved in senior center activities and to call the clinic.

The immediate problem was that she had just received a notification in the mail that her rent had been raised, and she did not know where she would get the money. She had gained 50 pounds in the last 2 years and was concerned about it. She said that aging was not the "golden years" she had thought it would be.

Mrs. Phillips arrived at the clinic by bus. In the intake interview she cried a great deal. Between periods of crying she sounded matter-of-fact and almost cheerful. She described problems in every aspect of her life. She has financial problems. Her husband, who had been self-employed as a housepainter, died 14 years ago, leaving her $2,000. Her Social Security and Supplemental Security Income payments were less than she had counted on. She did not know how she would make it. Most recently she had been running a cooking school in her home. At this time there was one pupil. She gave one of her cards to the therapist. It was grease-spotted and had battered corners. Mrs. Phillips had a brother in Phoenix but no other family. They had little contact. She married at age 39 and had no children. As she said, "They just didn't come."

She had a weight problem her entire life. About 1-1/2 years ago she attended Overeaters Anonymous. There she was told that she was anxious and stressed. They advised seeing a professional. Mrs. Phillips had not had a physical examination in over 10 years.

There was no previous history of psychiatric treatment. She was taking no medications but was using a variety of vitamins and health foods. As a consequence of the advice from someone at the talk radio station, Mrs. Phillips did join a senior center. She went on several bus trips with the group from the center, to Mexico and Las Vegas. She did not enjoy the trips because she believed that her roommate stole a jacket from her, and she did not plan on going again. She also bought a bicycle and signed up for an acting class.

Mrs. Phillips satisfied the criteria for major depressive disorder: dysphoric mood, significant weight gain, loss of energy, feelings of worthlessness, loss of interest, complaints of diminished ability to concentrate and remember, and excessive worrying. On intake screening, she scored 29 on the CES–D—well above the clinical cutoff—and 28 of 30 correct on the MMSE and 10 of 10 correct on the Mental Status Questionnaire, indicating absence of any cognitive impairment.

Additional psychological testing revealed an IQ of 106 on the WAIS–R, an MMPI profile with elevations on Scales 2 (*D*), 3 (*Hy*), 5 (*Mf*), and 6 (*Pa*), and a Brief Symptom Inventory (Derogatis & Spencer, 1982) with a global distress *t* score of 93 and elevations on depression, hostility, and psychoticism.

Conceptualization and treatment. Partly on the basis of having seen a large number of clients who presented similarly, the therapist and the clinical supervisor hypothesized that Mrs. Phillips had probably had a personality disorder her entire life, but she had been functional enough not to attract professional attention. We were impressed by the virtual absence of interpersonal commitments in her life. There seemed to have been little emotional tie to her husband and no history of intimate relationships before her marriage, which occurred at an advanced age, especially for that time. There was a pervasive vagueness to how she described her life, past and present. However, it seemed that it was only with the advent of her recent age-related problems that she was no longer able to manage, and she found herself with insufficient psychological resources. Therefore, she did genuinely become depressed.

Most writers describe personality disorders as decreasing in old age, although certain types of personalities—especially with narcissistic qualities—may have an especially difficult time adapting to the normative changes of later life (Goldstrom et al., 1987; LaRue et al., 1985). Thompson,

Gallagher, and Czirr (in press) discussed short-term therapy for depression in older patients with symptoms of personality disorder.

During the course of Mrs. Phillips's treatment, there was a constantly changing set of problems, primarily concerning money and sanitation. The one cooking student withdrew. Mrs. Phillips was concerned about the money and seemed to miss the student's company. The details of the student's life had given her something to talk about.

The therapist noted that Mrs. Phillips wore the same outfit to the clinic every week for the first 9 sessions. It was a purple cotton tent-style dress. She wore a different dress to the 10th session and a polyester knit pants suit to the 11th.

Mrs. Phillips described herself as a person who saved things she might need. She said her husband had called her a pack rat. For example, on Thursday afternoons she went to a nearby coffee shop to collect the food sections of any of that day's newspapers that had been left there. She clipped all of the grocery coupons and saved them. She often stocked up on products that were on special. Because of the volume of goods she was saving, including food as well as utensils and appliances for her cooking school, and because of being afraid that her bicycle might be stolen, she purchased a metal toolshed for her yard in which to store everything. When her collection outgrew it, she purchased two more. Other items were piled in the backyard with a plastic tablecloth laid over them and weighted down with concrete blocks. There were several encounters with neighbors about the appearance of the yard, followed by a complaint from the Department of Health.

The therapist made a home visit, at which time she observed the yard and noticed roaches in the kitchen. There was food—remnants of cheese, half a roll—on the kitchen table along with piles of cookbooks and clippings.

The initial treatment plan was cognitive–behavioral. Petunia's mood diary, however, kept drifting instead to lists of foods she was eating, as if she were reporting to Overeaters Anonymous.

The therapist taught Mrs. Phillips the strategy of breaking big insurmountable problems into little goals. Instead of organizing everything, she would just focus on clearing the kitchen table. Petunia liked that idea.

The therapist continued to encourage activity, as had been suggested earlier by the person at the radio station, discovering that it seemed to be more effective if she made suggestions paradoxically rather than directly (Herr & Weakland, 1979). Consistent with this observation, without urging specific action, the therapist reviewed with Mrs. Phillips the real problems she faced. Without arguing with Mrs. Phillips's choices, the therapist offered suggestions for avoiding the difficulties, such as encounters with the Health Department, and where to turn for assistance, such as the Social Security office.

By the end of treatment, Mrs. Phillips had made an appointment for a physical examination and had cleared her kitchen table.

Epilogue

The casebook concludes with an epilogue that discusses some final themes.

Ethics

Issues of personal autonomy, already discussed under mechanisms of change, lead directly to issues of ethics. It is generally recognized that voluntariness and informed consent can be compromised by frailty and dependency. Therefore, special care must be taken to involve older clients in determining treatment goals (O'Donahue, Fisher, & Krasner, 1987; Pratt, Schnell, & Wright, 1987). The subtlety of this problem in practice, however, was illustrated earlier by the question, Who is the client?

When dealing with demented elders, the most usual advice given to families and to service providers is to invite the demented individual to continue to make his or her own choices and to follow the principle of the least restrictive alternative, so long as there is no danger (Rabins & Mace, 1986). Again, in practice, maintaining this guideline can be difficult. The most frequent counterproductive consequence of well-intended helpers is inadvertently to undermine an older adult's autonomy by intervening too much (Kastenbaum, 1987).

Prevention

Psychological intervention with older adults can be organized in terms of target groups and levels of intervention (Smyer, Gatz, & Pruchno, in press). The target groups include individuals now old; families of frail elders (defined broadly to include social networks); and systemic concerns, from physical environment to public information to social policy considerations. Levels of interventions include remediation, secondary prevention, and primary prevention.

As has already been indicated, a developmental model of change applies to preventive interventions, and work with family caregivers is best seen as secondary prevention. More generally, the clinician is urged to remember the importance of prevention and to recognize that the most strategic intervention is the provision of education to all three target groups. A key issue for instruction is neither to confuse normal age-related change with disease nor to confuse disease with normal age-related change. Finally, in the current climate, providing facts on Alzheimer's disease takes on particular salience (see the Alzheimer's Disease Knowledge Test constructed by Dieckmann, Zarit, Zarit, & Gatz, 1988).

For More Information

For a clinical textbook on psychotherapy with older adults, see Knight's (1986) book. It covers most of the important themes from the viewpoint of a person actually working in a community mental health setting. For a book concerned only with dementia assessment and treatment, see Zarit, Orr, and Zarit's (1985) *The Hidden Victims of Alzheimer's Disease: Families Under Stress*. There are a variety of self-help books that can be read productively by therapists (although perhaps furtively) and given to patients or friends who ask about their parents. For example, for information on normal aging, see Skinner and Vaughan's (1983) *Enjoy Old Age: A Program of Self-Management*. For dementia, see Mace and Rabin's (1981) *The 36-Hour Day*. For more general concerns about aging parents, see Jarvik and Small's (1988) *Parentcaring: A Common Sense Guide for Adult Children*. I have also mentioned many other sources in this chapter.

PART 2: MENTAL HEALTH AND AGING IN PERSPECTIVE

In his master lecture on clinical geropsychology 10 years ago, Lawton (1978) complained that only an "occasional voice" decried "the inattention of clinical psychologists to the aged and the inattention of gerontologists to the traditional areas of clinical psychology." To give a sense of the magnitude of this problem of mutual neglect, Lawton asserted that he could have retrieved a couple of papers he wrote in 1968 and presented the same talk in 1978. This observation is no longer applicable in 1988. It is not possible to pull out notes from 1978 and use them today.

What has changed in the past decade? What is still in need of change? What changes can be expected in the next decade?

Changes

Five changes affect clinicians: (1) the increased number of older adults, coupled with society's increased awareness of aging; (2) psychologists' increased awareness of aging and related problems; (3) greater recognition of psychology under Medicare; (4) interest in Alzheimer's disease, a phenomenon that has emerged entirely within the past decade; and (5) the availability of empirical studies of psychotherapy with older adults.

1. The increase in the number of older Americans is detailed elsewhere in this volume. The percentage of the population that is aged 65 and older is creeping up; it was about 12.1% in 1986. The median age of the elderly population is increasing; men now aged 65 can expect to live

about another 15 years and women, 18 or 19 (AARP, 1987). Thus, the fastest-growing segment of the population are those aged 85 and older (Bureau of the Census, 1986). Since 1950, the number of those aged 65 and older has doubled, whereas the number aged 85 and older has increased fivefold (Bureau of the Census, 1987).

What is interesting about these numbers? For one thing, the 85 + age group is more likely to suffer from various chronic illnesses and frailties. Half have health-related difficulties leading to limitations of personal care (49%), home management (55%) activities, or both. Although at any given time, only 5% of older adults reside in institutions (Smyer, 1988), 24% of those aged 85 + live in group quarters, from rooming houses to nursing homes (Bureau of the Census, 1987).

The sex ratio is interesting because the predominance of women in the group called *aged* is so often overlooked. By age 85, for every 100 men there are 253 women (AARP, 1987). Furthermore, of all noninstitutionalized older women, 43% live alone. In brief, the demographic facts describe mental health risk factors. Physical illnesses, widowhood, and constrained living conditions constitute special stresses of later life.

2. These demographic shifts have led to increased public awareness of aging. In addition, psychologists have shown a heightened awareness of the demographic presence of older adults (Gatz & Pearson, 1988).

In June 1981, the Conference on Training Psychologists for Work in Aging was held in Boulder, Colorado (and therefore inevitably dubbed the "Older Boulder" conference; Santos & VandenBos, 1982). The conference recommended that all graduate programs in professional psychology include some training in aging and that more special programs or tracks in clinical psychology and aging be developed for students who wished to specialize. A motivating concern, both 10 years ago and today, is the insufficient number of psychologists providing health care delivery to the aged population. What has changed is that substantially more psychologists are expressing the concern.

The most recent data indicate that 6% of services provided by community mental health centers are to older adults (Flemming, Buchanan, Santos, & Rickards, 1984). A variety of estimates converge on 3% as the percentage of all private practice services that are provided to older adults by mental health professionals (Eisdorfer, 1987). Figures for psychologists tend to be lower than those for other providers (Smyer, 1988; Zarit, 1986). Smyer, Cohn, and Brannon (1988) described the neglect of nursing home consultation by psychologists.

Consistent with this picture of underservice, a number of surveys have shown that a very small number of clinical psychologists specialize in working with older adults. Three surveys scattered over the past decade have indicated that about two thirds of all practitioners *never* see an older client (Dye, 1978; Turner & Turner, 1987; VandenBos, Stapp, & Kilburg, 1981). Stapp, Tucker, and VandenBos (1985) estimated that there were 160 professional psychologists specializing in services to older adults and another 1,400 who saw at least some aged clients.

My recent perusal of the 1987 *National Register of Health Service Providers in Psychology* (Council for the National Register of Health Service Providers in Psychology, 1987) revealed a similar estimate. A sampling of every nth page showed that 13% of these providers specified persons aged 65 + as among the clients they served or presumably would be willing to serve. In other words, some 1,982 professional psychologists either do or would see older clients.

3. It seems likely that the increased attention of psychologists has also been influenced by the prospects, recently rewarded, of including psychologists as providers who could be reimbursed under Medicare. In 1978 Lawton concluded the following:

> The intrinsic appeal of professional work with the aging is not great enough in itself to stimulate an unusual degree of growth in [clinical geropsychology]. The financial incentive of service reimbursement for the clinician in private practice and for the mental-health-agency employers of clinicians is a necessary condition of growth.

Recognition of the professional standing of psychologists in Medicare has not kept pace with regulations concerning psychologists in other health care reimbursement systems. For this reason, it has been a target of efforts by various individuals, such as Tom Stein of West Virginia (Buie, 1988a), and through the American Psychological Association's Practice Directorate. There are many other problems with Medicare, including biases against mental health services in general, against preventive services of all types, and against any sort of long-term care for chronic conditions. In this instance, the self-interest of psychologists would seem to coincide with at least some of the interests of aged persons.

Inpatient mental health services, reimbursed under Medicare Part A, are limited to a lifetime total of 190 days. Outpatient mental health services, included under Part B, have a 50–50 copayment rate (in contrast to 80–20 for physical health care services), and there has been a $250 annual limit. In the past, psychologists could be reimbursed only for diagnostic testing, so long as the testing was by physician referral. The only way psychologists could be paid for psychotherapy was if a physician referred the patient, supervised the service by being in the facility at the same time, and paid the psychologist's fee (Uyeda, 1986).

Congress has passed a bill, effective in 1988, that allows reimbursing psychologists for services provided independently of physicians at rural health clinics and community mental health centers (Buie, 1988b) and quadrupling the annual limit. Lobbying for full recognition will continue into the next decade.

4. Alzheimer's disease, virtually unmentioned a decade ago, has emerged into striking prominence, from media attention to allocations of funds for research support. It seems likely that one by-product has been increased attention by psychologists, especially those interested in neuropsychology. For community psychologists, too, a fascinating phenomenon has been the evolution of a small social movement in the form of networks of relatives of dementia patients (especially the Alzheimer's Disease and Related Disorders Association). Perhaps the aspect that has captured the most attention of clinicians has been research and services concerning family caregivers of dementing elders, and the literature in this area has simply exploded.

The general public is certainly aware of Alzheimer's disease. Recently a colleague of mine took his son to an Old Timers game at Dodger Stadium. The son, believing that his father had said "Alzheimer's game," was stunned by how well the men played. The Saunders case illustrates the phenomenon as well.

5. The fifth change is the emergence of empirical studies of psychotherapy with older adults. Ten years ago there was little literature on psychotherapy with older adults. What there was often presented the rationale for why a particular theory should be relevant (whether Jungian or behavior therapy), but then it concluded, sadly, that there was no empirical evaluation of any of these therapies. Lawton (1978) referred to the "armchair quality of [the] thinking" in much of the literature.

The situation has changed. A number of scholars are now very invested in studying psychotherapy with older adults, and research programs are becoming more sophisticated. Paralleling the evolution of controlled research on psychotherapy outcome with younger adults, the bulk of empirical work with aged clients has been directed toward cognitive and behavioral intervention, with depressed elders the most frequent target of treatment. The three most systematic efforts are those of Jarvik and Steuer at the University of California, Los Angeles, Gallagher and Thompson at the Palo Alto Veterans Administration Hospital, and Beutler and others at Arizona Health Sciences Center (Thompson et al., 1986). Those scholars have found older adults to be highly responsive to therapy, group and individual. Similarly, the quality of the conceptualizations and the program evaluations of community interventions with aged persons has improved (Smyer & Gatz, 1983). There are also numerous examples of controlled evaluations of psychological interventions with family caregivers of dementia patients (Haley, Brown, & Levine, 1987; Zarit, Anthony, & Boutselis, 1987). Also see review chapters in Smyer, Zarit, and Qualls (in press) and Gatz, Bengtson, and Blum (in press).

Certainly the examples cited here are exceptions, and more well-designed empirical work, including defining the psychopathological population and explicating the rationale for the intervention, is needed over the next decade.

Nonchanges

Along with these five changes are three issues that have remained relatively unchanged. These include (1) insufficient graduate training opportunities, (2) rhetoric about negative attitudes as a barrier to service provision, and (3) controversy concerning continuity and discontinuity when working with older adults compared with other age groups.

1. Despite the Older Boulder conference recommendations, there remains a need to expand graduate training opportunities. Although there is no formal identification of programs, basically there is only a handful of universities that offer specialized graduate training in clinical psychology and aging. At least one reason is insufficient availability of training grant support. More optimistically, nearly a half of internships listed by the Association of Psychological Internship Centers offer a rotation in geriatrics, with Veterans Administration funding undoubtedly playing an encouraging role. In addition, a recent survey of participants in the Older Boulder conference (Santos & Dawson, 1989) indicated that there are more courses within established clinical and counseling training programs, so that an interested and motivated student could more readily gain some exposure. The topic of training opportunities should be revisited in the next decade and progress pushed for in the meantime.

2. Negative stereotypes and prejudicial attitudes about aged people by practitioners continue to be cited as a barrier to older adults' obtaining mental health services (Lasoski, 1986; Roybal, 1988), with some research supporting a preference for treating younger rather than older clients (Ray, McKinney, & Ford, 1987). Research, however, tends to substantiate that treatment biases reflect diagnostic category more than age (Hochman, Storandt, & Rosenberg, 1986). Gatz and Pearson (1988) have also maintained that negative stereotypes should be examined substantively rather than condemned outright. Some stereotypes do have bases in fact and represent the complexity of the older adult's psychological situation.

Complementing the presumed lack of interest by psychological practitioners in older clients is the avoidance by older adults of mental health service providers (Lasoski & Thelen, 1987; Roybal, 1988). In fact, a provocative book by Brody (1985) exquisitely documents the extent to which older adults experience psychological distress as well as physical pain but do not report physical or mental health symptoms to anyone, let alone to a medical or psychological professional.

Reluctance to consult a mental health professional is often attributed to cohort (Lawton, 1978), and it has been predicted that older adults in future generations who grow up in a more psychologically sophisticated era will be more willing to seek professional help. If this interpretation is correct, change should be apparent fairly soon, perhaps by 10 years from now. If reluctance persists, then the cohort interpretation should be reexamined.

Meanwhile, the nature and extent of the presumed reluctance has been questioned (e.g., Knight, 1986). Similar to Knight's experience in a community mental health center, my colleagues and I have found that older adults and their families do take advantage of psychological services offered in our training clinic when such services are made available to them and when such services are perceived as truly meeting their needs.

3. A third issue that has seemingly maintained itself over the past decade concerns continuity versus discontinuty (i.e., the relative amount of focus on similarities versus differences in psychotherapy with older adults and with other age groups). My colleagues and I find ourselves closer to the continuity than to the discontinuity position (Gatz et al., 1985). Furthermore, the greater discontinuity may be in the area of assessment than in the area of psychotherapeutic treatment (e.g., see Knight, 1986; Zarit, Eiler, & Hassinger, 1985).

Those who write about differences in psychotherapy with older adults most often suggest modifications such as adaptations to physical limitations (Zeiss & Lewinsohn, 1986), such as the use of large print materials (Gallagher & Thompson, 1981); shorter treatment (Brink, 1979); use of role induction (Knight, 1986); more structure (Gallagher & Thompson, 1981) or therapist activity (Newton et al., 1986); greater care about which defenses to challenge (Sadavoy & Leszcz, 1987); more application of life review techniques (Haight, 1988); gradual termination (Newton et al., 1986; Thompson et al., 1986); and more use of community resources (Knight, 1986; Newton et al., 1986). The difficulty, as Kastenbaum (1987) has also suggested, is that such assertions may lack both careful examination of their premises and empirical evaluation of their application.

The continuity argument would maintain that, on the whole, modifications follow directly from integrating knowledge of life span development, normative life events, and normal age-related changes with what the astute clinician already knows and practices. To the extent that there are adaptations to be made, they have their basis more in the particular client and the particular attribute inspiring the adaptation (from visual impairment to lack of familiarity with psychotherapy) than in chronological age per se. The casebook illustrates this approach.

Prospects for the Next Decade

Four themes would likely be included in a master lecture on psychology and aging 10 years from now: (1) demographic changes, (2) availability of graduate training opportunities, (3) responsivity to the importance of physical health problems of older adults to their emotional well-being, and (4) reimbursement of providers for psychological services to older adults.

1. Just as attention to the demographic revolution represented a change between 1978 and the present, in 10 years demographics will still be creating attention for the aged population. In 10 years the number of aged persons will not yet have peaked, but by 2010 the first of the baby boomers will start reaching age 65, and by then 18% of those aged 65 and older could themselves have a living parent (Bureau of the Census, 1987). In other words, adult children may frequently be caring for aged parents after their own retirement.

2. Growth in training programs was represented as a nonchange between 1978 and today. Student interest in aging will gradually force changes in training programs. In response to student demand, more graduate programs will actively seek to hire faculty trained in clinical psychology and aging, courses wil be established, and at clinical faculty meetings the idea of requiring a course on aging for all students will be discussed, just as the Older Boulder conference recommended.

3. The review of demographics and the examples in the casebook made clear how prominent chronic health problems are in the lives of older persons. Over the next decade health psychology will grow, gerontologists and health psychologists will notice their common ground, and they will create more interchange in relation to both research and professional roles. Siegler's (1988) master lecture on health in this series on adult development and aging could be called the first step toward the next decade (see the chapter "Developmental Health Psychology," by I. C. Siegler in this volume).

4. Continuing the theme of health and caregiving, it is hoped that public awareness will translate into political pressure and that in 10 years the nation will have some sort of long-term care insurance plan. Remembering the limitations of Medicare, I can only predict that mental health needs will not be sufficiently acknowledged and that psychologists will not have parity with physicians.

References

AARP. (1987). *A profile of older Americans*. Washington, DC: American Association of Retired Persons.

Alafuzoff, I., Iqbal, K., Friden, H., Adolfsson, R., & Winblad, B. (1987). Histopathological criteria for progressive dementia disorders: Clinical-pathological correlation and classification by multivariate data analysis. *Acta Neuropathologica, 74*, 209–225.

American Psychiatric Association. (1980). *Diagnostic and statistical manual of mental disorders* (3rd ed.). Washington, DC: Author.

Anthony-Bergstone, C. R., Zarit, S. H., & Gatz, M. (1988). Symptoms of psychological distress among caregivers of dementia patients. *Psychology and Aging, 3*, 245–248.

Baltes, P. B., & Danish, S. (1980). Intervention in lifespan development and aging: Issues and concepts. In R. R. Turner & H. W. Reese (Eds.), *Lifespan developmental psychology: Intervention*. New York: Academic Press.

Bengtson, V. L., & Kuypers, J. A. (1985). The family support cycle: Psychosocial issues in the aging family. In J. M. A. Munnichs, P. Mussen, & E. Olbrich (Eds.), *Life span and change in a gerontological perspective* (pp. 257–273). New York: Academic Press.

Blazer, D., Hughes, D. C., & George, L. K. (1987). The epidemiology of depression in an elderly community population. *Gerontologist, 27,* 281–287.

Brink, T. L. (1979). *Geriatric psychotherapy*. New York: Human Sciences Press.

Brody, E. M. (1985). *Mental and physical health practices of older people*. New York: Springer Publishing.

Brust, J. C. M. (1988). Vascular dementia is overdiagnosed. *Archives of Neurology, 45,* 799–801.

Buie, J. (1988a, May). Rain fails to mar its day in the sun. *APA Monitor,* pp. 20–21.

Buie, J. (1988b, June). Red tape delays reimbursements under Medicare. *APA Monitor,* p. 14.

Burns, D. (1981). *Feeling good*. New York: Signet Books.

Bureau of the Census. (1986, December). *Age structure of the U.S. population in the 21st century* (DC Statistical Brief SB-1-86). Washington, DC: U.S. Government Printing Office.

Bureau of the Census. (1987, September). *America's centenarians, current population reports, special studies* (DC Series P-23, No. 153). Washington, DC: U.S. Government Printing Office.

National Register of Health Service Providers in Psychology. (1987). Washington, DC: Council for the National Register of Health Service Providers in Psychology.

Derogatis, L. R., & Spencer, P. M. (1982). *The Brief Symptom Inventory (BSI): Administration and procedures manual 1*. Baltimore, MD: Johns Hopkins University School of Medicine, Clinical Psychometric Research Unit.

Dieckmann, L., Zarit, S. H., Zarit, J. M., & Gatz, M. (1988). Alzheimer's Disease Knowledge Test. *Gerontologist, 28,* 402–408.

Dye, C. J. (1978). Psychologists' role in the provision of mental health care for the elderly. *Professional Psychology, 9,* 38–49.

Eisdorfer, C. (1987, March 31). Testimony presented at a hearing on the re-authorization of the Older Americans Act.

Erikson, E. (1963). *Childhood and society* (2nd ed.). New York: Norton.

Felton, B. J. (1982). The aged. In L. Snowden (Ed.), *Reaching the underserved: Mental health needs of neglected populations*. San Francisco: Jossey-Bass.

Flavell, J. H. (1963). *The developmental psychology of Jean Piaget*. Princeton, NJ: Van Nostrand.

Flemming, A. S., Buchanan, J. G., Santos, J. F., & Rickards, L. D. (1984). *Mental health services for the elderly: Report on a survey of community mental health centers*. Washington, DC: Action Committee to Implement the Mental Health Recommendations of the 1981 White House Conference on Aging.

Folstein, J. E., Folstein, S. E., & McHugh, P. R. (1975). Mini-Mental State: A practical method for grading the cognitive state of patients for the clinician. *Journal of Psychiatric Research, 12,* 189–198.

Gallagher, D., & Thompson, L. W. (1981). *Depression in the elderly: A behavioral treatment manual*. Los Angeles: University of Southern California Press.

Gatz, M., Bengtson, V. L., & Blum, M. J. (in press). Caregiving families. In J. E. Birren & K. W. Schaie (Eds.), *Handbook of the psychology of aging* (3rd ed.). New York: Academic Press.

Gatz, M., & Pearson, C. G. (1988). Ageism revised and the provision of psychological services. *American Psychologist, 43*, 184–188.

Gatz, M., Popkin, S., Pino, C. D., & VandenBos, G. R. (1985). Psychological interventions with older adults. In J. E. Birren & K. W. Schaie (Eds.), *Handbook of the psychology of aging* (2nd ed., pp. 775–785). New York: Van Nostrand Reinhold.

George, L. K., & Gwyther, L. P. (1986). Caregiver well-being: A multidimensional examination of family caregivers of demented adults. *Gerontologist, 26*, 253–259.

Goldstrom, I. D., Burns, B., Kessler, L. G., Feueberg, M. A., Larson, D. B., Miller, N. E., & Cromer, W. J. (1987). Mental health services use by elderly adults in a primary care setting. *Journal of Gerontology, 42*, 147–153.

Gutmann, D., Griffith, B., & Grunes, J. (1982). Developmental contributions to the late-onset affective disorders. In P. B. Baltes and O. Brim (Eds.), *Lifespan development and behavior* (Vol. 4). New York: Academic Press.

Haight, B. K. (1988). The therapeutic role of a structured life review process in homebound elderly subjects. *Journal of Gerontology: Psychological Sciences, 43*, 40–44.

Haley, S. L., Brown, L., & Levine, E. G. (1987). Experimental evaluation of the effectiveness of group intervention for dementia caregivers. *Gerontologist, 27*, 376–382.

Herr, J. J., & Weakland, J. H. (1979). *Counseling elders and their families.* New York: Springer Publishing.

Hochman, L. O., Storandt, M., & Rosenberg, A. M. (1986). Age and its effect on perceptions of psychopathology. *Psychology and Aging, 1*, 337–338.

Jarvik, L., & Small, G. (1988). *Parentcaring: A common sense guide for adult children.* New York: Crown.

Kahn, R. L., Goldfarb, A. I., Pollack, M., & Peck, A. (1960). Brief objective measures for the determination of mental status in the aged. *American Journal of Psychiatry, 117*, 326–328.

Karuza, J., Rabinowitz, V. C., & Zevon, M. A. (1986). Implications of control and responsibility on helping the aged. In M. M. Baltes & P. B. Baltes (Eds.), *The psychology of control and aging* (pp. 373–396). Hillsdale, NJ: Erlbaum.

Kastenbaum, R. (1987). Prevention of age-related problems. In L. L. Carstensen & B. A. Edelstein (Eds.), *Handbook of clinical gerontology* (pp. 322–334). Oxford, England: Pergamon Press.

Kermis, M. D. (1986). The epidemiology of mental disorder in the elderly: A response to the Senate/AARP report. *Gerontologist, 26*, 482–487.

Kirby, H. B., & Harper, R. G. (1988). Team assessment of geriatric mental patients: II. Behavioral dynamics and psychometric testing in the diagnosis of functional dementia due to hysterical behavior. *Gerontologist, 28*, 260–262.

Knight, B. (1986). *Psychotherapy with older adults.* Beverly Hills, CA: Sage.

LaRue, A., Dessonville, C., & Jarvik, L. F. (1985). Aging and mental disorders. In J. E. Birren & K. W. Schaie (Eds.), *Handbook of the psychology of aging* (2nd ed., pp. 664–702). New York: Van Nostrand Reinhold.

Lasoski, M. C. (1986). Reasons for low utilization of mental health services by the elderly. In T. L. Brink (Ed.), *Clinical gerontology: A guide to assessment and intervention*. New York: Haworth Press.

Lasoski, M. C., & Thelen, M. H. (1987). Attitudes of older and middle-aged persons toward mental health intervention. *Gerontologist, 27*, 288–292.

Lawton, M. P. (1978, August). *Clinical geropsychology: Problems and prospects*. Master Lecture presented at the 86th Annual Convention of the American Psychological Association, Toronto, Ontario, Canada.

Levinson, D. J. (1978). *The seasons of a man's life*. New York: Knopf.

Lewis, M. I., & Butler, R. N. (1974). Life-review therapy: Putting memories to work in individual and group psychotherapy. *Geriatrics, 29*, 165–173.

Lieberman, M. A., & Tobin, S. S. (1983). *The experience of old age*. New York: Basic Books.

Mace, N. L., & Rabins, P. V. (1981). *The 36-hour day*. Baltimore, MD: Johns Hopkins University Press.

Mahoney, M. J. (1981, August). *Psychotherapy and human change processes*. Master Lecture presented at the 89th Annual Convention of the American Psychological Association, Los Angeles.

Neale, J. M., Oltmanns, T. F., & Davison, G. C. (1982). *Case studies in abnormal psychology*. New York: Wiley.

Nemiroff, R. A., & Colarusso, C. A. (1985). *The race against time: Psychotherapy and psychoanalysis in the second half of life*. New York: Plenum Press.

Newton, N. A., Brauer, D., Gutmann, D. L., & Grunes, J. (1986). Psychodynamic therapy with the aged: A review. In T. L. Brink (Ed.), *Clinical gerontology: A guide to assessment and intervention* (pp. 205–229). New York: Haworth Press.

O'Donahue, W. T., Fisher, J. E., & Krasner, L. (1987). Ethics and the elderly. In L. L. Carstensen & B. A. Edelstein (Eds.), *Handbook of clinical gerontology* (pp. 322–334). Oxford, England: Pergamon Press.

Post, F. (1987). Paranoid and schizophrenic disorders among the aging. In L. L. Carstensen & B. A. Edelstein (Eds.), *Handbook of clinical gerontology* (pp. 43–56). Oxford, England: Pergamon Press.

Pratt, C., Schnell, V., & Wright, S. (1987). Ethical concerns of family caregivers to dementia patients. *Gerontologist, 27*, 632–638.

Pruchno, R. A., Blow, F. C., Smyer, M. A. (1984). Life events and interdependent lives. *Human Development, 27*, 31–41.

Rabins, P. V., & Mace, N. L. (1986). Some ethical issues in dementia care. In T. L. Brink (Ed.), *Clinical gerontology: A guide to assessment and intervention* (pp. 503–512). New York: Haworth Press.

Radloff, L. S. (1977). The CES–D Scale: A self-report depression scale for research in the general populations. *Applied Psychological Measurement, 1*, 385–401.

Ray, D. C., McKinney, K. A., & Ford, C. V. (1987). Differences in psychologists' ratings of older and younger clients. *Gerontologist, 27*, 82–86.

Riegel, K. (1976). The dialectics of human development. *American Psychologist, 31*, 689–700.

Rodin, J. (1980). Managing the stress of aging: The role of control and coping. In H. Ursin & S. Levine (Eds.), *Coping and health* (pp. 171–202). New York: Academic Press.

Roybal, E. R. (1988). Mental health and aging: The need for an expanded federal response. *American Psychologist, 43*, 189–194.

Sadavoy, J., & Leszcz, M. (Eds.). (1987). *Treating the elderly with psychotherapy: The scope for change in later life.* New York: International Universities Press.

Santos, J. F., & VandenBos, G. R. (Eds.). (1982). *Psychology and the older adult: Challenges for training in the 1980s.* Washington, DC: American Psychological Association.

Santos, J. F., & Dawson, G. D. (1989). *Survey of APA members at Older Boulder, the 1981 Conference on Training Psychologists to Work in Aging.*

Sarton, M. (1973). *As we are now.* New York: Norton.

Schaie, K. W. (1988). Ageism in psychological research. *American Psychologist, 43,* 179–183.

Scogin, F., Hamblin, D., & Beutler, L. (1987). Bibliotherapy for depressed older adults: A self-help alternative. *Gerontologist, 27,* 383–387.

Shapiro, D. (1965). *Neurotic styles.* New York: Basic Books.

Shapiro, D. (1981). *Autonomy and rigid character.* New York: Basic Books.

Sherman, E. (1981). *Counseling the aged.* New York: Free Press.

Sherman, E. (1987). Reminiscence groups for community elderly. *Gerontologist, 27,* 569–572.

Skinner, B. F., & Vaughan, E. (1983). *Enjoy old age: A program of self-management.* New York: Warner Books.

Slivinske, L. R., & Fitch, V. L. (1987). The effect of control enhancing interventions on the well-being of elderly individuals living in retirement communities. *Gerontologist, 27,* 176–181.

Smith, M. B. (1968). Competence and socialization. In J. A. Clausen (Ed.), *Socialization and society* (pp. 270–320). Boston: Little, Brown.

Smyer, M. A. (1987). Life transitions and aging: Implications for counseling older adults. *Counseling Psychologist, 12,* 17–28.

Smyer, M. A. (1988, August). *Nursing homes as a setting for psychological practice: Public policy perspectives.* Paper presented at the 96th Annual Convention of the American Psychological Association, Atlanta, GA.

Smyer, M. A., Cohn, M. D., & Brannon, D. (1988). *Mental health consultation in nursing homes.* New York: New York University Press.

Smyer, M., & Gatz, M. (Eds.). (1983). *Mental health and aging: Programs and evaluations.* Beverly Hills, CA: Sage.

Smyer, M., Gatz, M., & Pruchno, R. A. (in press). Community psychology and aging. In M. S. Gibbs, J. R. Lachenmeyer, & J. Sigal (Eds.), *Community psychology.* New York: Gardner Press.

Smyer, M. A., Zarit, S. H., & Qualls, S. H. (1988). Psychological intervention with the aging individual. In J. E. Birren & K. W. Schaie (Eds.), *Handbook of the psychology of aging* (3rd ed.). New York: Academic Press.

Stapp, J., Tucker, A., & VandenBos, G. R. (1985). Census of psychological personnel: 1983. *American Psychologist, 40,* 1317–1351.

Teri, L., & Gallagher, D. (in press). Cognitive behavioral interventions for depressed patients with dementia of the Alzheimer's type. In T. Sunderland (Ed.), *Depression in Alzheimer's disease: Component or consequence?* New York: Grune & Stratton.

Teri, L., & Reifler, B. V. (1987). Depression and dementia. In L. L. Carstensen & B. A. Edelstein (Eds.), *Handbook of clinical gerontology* (pp. 112–119). Oxford, England: Pergamon Press.

Thompson, L. W., Davies, R., Gallagher, D., & Krantz, S. E. (1986). Cognitive therapy with older adults. In T. L. Brink (Ed.), *Clinical gerontology: A guide to assessment and intervention* (pp. 245–279). New York: Haworth Press.

Thompson, L. W., Gallagher, D., & Breckenridge, J. S. (1987). Comparative effectiveness of psychotherapies for depressed elders. *Journal of Consulting and Clinical Psychology, 55*, 385–390.

Thompson, L. W., Gallagher, D., & Czirr, R. (in press). Personality disorders and outcome in the treatment of late-life depression. *Journal of Geriatric Psychiatry.*

Tobin, S. (1986, November). *Social workers' perceptions of elderly clients.* Paper presented at the annual meeting of the Gerontological Society of America, Chicago.

Turner, B. F., & Turner, C. B. (1987). Percentages of elderly in psychotherapists' practices in the mid-1980s. *Adult Development and Aging Newsletter, 15*(2), 11–12.

Uyeda, M. (1986, August). *Medicare for psychologists.* Paper presented at the 94th Annual Convention of the American Psychological Association, Washington, DC.

VandenBos, G. R., Stapp, J., & Kilburg, R. R. (1981). Health service providers in psychology. *American Psychologist, 36*, 1395–1418.

Watzlawick, P., Weakland, J., & Fisch, R. (1974). *Change: Principles of problem formation and problem resolution.* New York: Norton.

Zarit, S. H. (1986, fall). Application of clinical psychology to the problems of aging. *Clinical Psychologist, 39*, 95–96.

Zarit, S. H., Anthony, C. R., & Boutselis, M. (1987). Interventions with caregivers of dementia patients: Comparison of two approaches. *Psychology and Aging, 2*, 225–232.

Zarit, S. H., Eiler, J., & Hassinger, M. (1985). Clinical assessment. In J. E. Birren & K. W. Schaie (Eds.), *Handbook of the psychology of aging* (2nd ed., pp. 725–754). New York: Van Nostrand Reinhold.

Zarit, S. H., Orr, N., & Zarit, J. M. (1985). *The hidden victims of Alzheimer's disease: Families under stress.* New York: New York University Press.

Zarit, S. H., Reever, K. E., & Bach-Peterson, J. (1981). Relatives of the impaired elderly: Correlates of feelings of burden. *Gerontologist, 21*, 158–164.

Zeiss, A. M., & Lewinsohn, P. M. (1986, fall). Adapting behavioral treatment for depression to meet the needs of the elderly. *Clinical Psychologist, 39*, 98–100.

ILENE C. SIEGLER

DEVELOPMENTAL HEALTH PSYCHOLOGY

I lene C. Siegler is associate professor of medical psychology in the Department of Psychiatry at the Duke University School of Medicine and is affiliated with the Duke University Behavioral Medicine Research Center. Her major research interests are personality predictors of coronary disease and the interactions of health and disease with normal aging.

Siegler has written more than 70 publications, including *Federal Age Discrimination in Employment Law* (written with Charles D. Edelman), and she coedited the first volume of *Clinical Psychology of Aging*. She is currently a consulting editor of *Psychology and Aging* and *Behavioral Medicine Abstracts* and sits on the editorial boards of *Journal of Gerontology: Psychological Sciences*, *The Gerontologist*, and *Experimental Aging Research*. She was also an associate editor of the *Encyclopedia of Aging*.

A past president of the Division of Adult Development and Aging of the American Psychological Association, she is active in the Gerontological Society and other professional groups, and she has made presentations at numerous meetings and colloquia. She has served as a consultant on academic and government projects dealing with the aging population.

Siegler received a PhD in developmental psychology from Syracuse University and an MPH in epidemiology from the University of North Carolina.

DEVELOPMENTAL HEALTH PSYCHOLOGY

What Is Developmental Health Psychology?

Developmental health psychology is the study of the three-way interaction of health, behavior, and aging. Such study attempts to answer questions like, What is normal aging, and how is it different from disease? Typically, a developmental health psychologist, working from longitudinal studies of normally aged persons, studies the impact of age and health behavior on various diseases common in middle and later life (such as coronary disease and Alzheimer's disease). He or she also draws information from health psychology, behavioral medicine, and geriatric medicine, in order to better understand the aging process.

Setting the Context

It is important to define age groups when one is discussing health, behavior, and aging. Adulthood starts at roughly age 25, the age at which most physiological processes are fully developed and are still functioning at close to peak efficiency. Adulthood, then, continues through *middle age* (roughly age 45) into *later life* (at 65) and into *old age* (those 85 and older). Note the division of those over age 65 into two groups. The extension of life expectancy in this century has led to this distinction, and it is an important one for developmental health psychologists. Those in later life may require different services than those in old age.

Brody, Brock, and Williams (1987) illustrated the significance of the lengthening of life in a way that caught my attention that the traditional catechism—"In 1910, 4% of the population was over 65, whereas by 1980, 11% of the population was over 65"—never did. They stated, "[I]n 1900 only 25% of the persons in the U.S. lived beyond age 65, while by 1985 approximately 70% survived until age 65 and 30% lived to be 80 or more. If present trends continue almost half of all deaths will occur after age 80" (p. 211). This states the case in terms of individuals. It conveys the message that not only are there more older persons, but they are older than in previous generations.

A central issue related to extreme aging is the extent to which the additional years of life are spent healthy and functional versus time spent disabled and dysfunctional. The data for making such a calculation are weak. Brody et al. (1987), however, speculated that for each "good year" (that is, healthy year) added to an individual's life, an additional 3.5 "compromised years" are added. These are straight-line demographic projections and thus an extremely conservative estimate that does not take into account any possible research findings about changes that may improve the health of the elderly population (T. F. Williams, personal communication, October 3, 1988).

This aspect of the aging U.S. population is significant for psychologists who provide services to elderly patients because it means that such professionals will increasingly need to know more about physical aging, the differences between normal aging and disease, and the interrelationship (and differential diagnosis) of physical and mental problems. Developmental health psychology thus provides basic and applied research paradigms for the clinical psychology of later life.

This chapter continues a 30-year history of interest in health, behavior, and aging. Jones (1959) focused on understanding shifts in mortality in the 20th century. Welford and Birren (1965) gave the physiological psychology of aging a major place in our thinking. Eisdorfer and Wilkie (1977) used stress as the organizing principle to discuss health–behavior relationships. Siegler and Costa (1985) reviewed the findings about psychological functioning where *normally aging* persons (defined as those without a specific diagnosis) were compared with their less healthy peers; they focused on the impact of health or disease on behavior as

The author's work on this chapter has been supported in part by Grant POI HL36587 from the National Heart, Lung, and Blood Institute, and POI AG05128 from the National Institute of Aging.

The author would particularly like to thank Merril F. Elias, John B. Nowlin, Karen Hooker, Michelle Rusin, and Noel Solomons for their comments on this chapter, and Peggy Edwards for secretarial assistance.

well as the effect of behavior on health outcomes. Elias, Elias, and Elias (in press) provide a review of the literature since 1984, with attention to both sides of the health–behavior relationship. They review studies that focus on behavioral factors as both predictors and consequences of major chronic diseases (cardiovascular disorders, hypertension, diabetes, and the dementias). Finally, longitudinal studies of normally aging persons that started in the mid-1950s have long-term participants now reaching the century mark, providing new data on the *oldest old* and illustrating the strengths and weaknesses of our traditional approaches. For example, because any specific disease is a relatively rare event, even in the elderly, it is difficult to study specific disease outcomes with existing samples.

Some Preliminary Comments

Before reviewing specific research issues and findings, I would like to state some assumptions and observations that influence my own view of developmental health psychology.

1. Normal aging is not the same thing as disease, although it may be more difficult to make the distinction at extreme old ages. This distinction is particularly important in terms of clinical practice and public policy. If an older person's problem is defined as a physical disease, then we expect the geriatric physician to be able to cure it. If, on the other hand, the problem is one of management and coping, the more appropriate health professional to provide assistance is a psychologist.

Rowe and Kahn (1987) made an important contribution to gerontology by restating the aging versus disease controversy in terms of risk factor modification. Successfully aging persons in this formulation have different risk factor profiles. These risk factor profiles are related to extrinsic or behavioral aging (rather than intrinsic biological aging) and thus can be modified by changes in behaviors. They call for health promotion and disease prevention interventions, techniques that are central to health psychologists.

For the researcher, the distinction between normal aging and disease can have major effects on conclusions. It can also be difficult to define. Consider, for example, data on heart disease from the Baltimore Longitudinal Study (Lakatta, 1987). With traditional epidemiological screening tools (history of angina pectoris or heart attack and an abnormal electrocardiogram), about 50% of those older persons with verified heart disease (based on autopsy evidence of diseased coronary arteries) were identified. Only when people were evaluated under the stress of exercise, with electrocardiographic monitoring and thallium scanning to observe the heart muscle, were the remainder identified. This leaves for study a group of older adults in whom "cardiovascular function does not markedly deteriorate with age" (p. 191). Thus our definition of disease may depend on technological innovation, available funds, and the willingness of apparently "healthy" persons to undergo detailed diagnostic procedures.

2. Health and illness are not inverses of each other. The concepts of "health" and "illness" are as much hypothetical constructs as are many psychological constructs. How we define and measure health and what we use as indices of disease are critical for progress in researching this area. Psychologists have major methodological contributions to make in this regard because we understand the way people perceive, understand, and interpret their symptoms, as well as the basic processes of remembering and categorization, which are probably crucial to such definitions. We also represent the profession expert in measurement and the development of scales.

Although life satisfaction, for example, has a clearly demonstrated association with physical health (Okun & Stock, 1987), it is overused as an outcome variable for older adults. Often correlations between objective circumstances and psychological well-being are weak. In a study of older persons with common chronic diseases (arthritis, ischemic heart disease, chronic pulmonary disease, diabetes mellitus, and cancer), physicians underestimated quality of life compared with the older persons' reports (Pearlman & Uhlmann, 1988). Older persons appear to cognitively manipulate their perceptions to maintain appropriate psychological well-being in the face of imperfect circumstances.

3. Developmental health psychology requires collaboration with other disciplines. The physiology and clinical course of each disorder study must be understood for the behavioral research to make sense. For work to progress, models must be consistent with the current state of medical and sociological, as well as psychological, knowledge. With respect to practice, this does not mean that all treatment must be done from a "team" approach with a physician as the captain. It does mean that the provider of psychological services to the older adult needs to know about more topics and that there will be a greater need to collaborate in, or coordinate treatment with, other professionals.

4. Geriatric medicine focuses on a number of specific disorders that are of relatively low prevalence or produce little disability in younger people. Minaker and Rowe (1985) reviewed five major geriatric syndromes that lead to patient referrals: memory failure, urinary incontinence, falls, systolic hypertension, and polypharmacy. There are clear and obvious roles for psychologists to play in the assessment and treatment, as well as research, of each of these. For example, behavioral treatments may be highly effective for the treatment of urinary incontinence. Psychological principles may be most useful in modifying dietary and exercise practices to reduce hypertension. Assertiveness training may be necessary to modify patient–physician interactions that contribute to polypharmacy and its associated negative effects due to drug interactions (Storandt, 1983).

5. The psychology of aging is different from the psychology of death, although it is certainly true that death ends aging. Although the study of dying and death is important in its own right, I am more concerned in this chapter with the predictors of mortality and the extent to which age at death is an important index of the overall health of an individual or population and is an index of the conduct of a society.

The Role of Age in Developmental Health Psychology

A basic question in developmental health psychology is, When a person's age is known, what does one know about that individual's health? Given the date the question was asked, one knows the individual's date of birth by subtraction. This reveals the person's birth cohort and makes possible a set of assumptions (e.g., public health or immunizations programs in effect during childhood) that can then be tested in interaction with the individual. Assumptions based on birth cohort alone are inadequate; they must be tempered by information about, for example, the person's sex, social class, and place of origin (Rosow, 1978). Probability of exposure to a disease is an important concern. Consider the current example of AIDS: one would want to know the individual's sexual preference and geographical location.

In addition to the information provided by the individual's birth cohort and sociohistorical probable life story (obtained by interview), there are some general "rules" that relate to the age of the person:

1. Disease is more common in elderly people. The average older person has 3.5 diseases and fills 13 prescriptions annually (Albert, 1989).

2. Most of the common diseases in later life do not start there; thus a life span developmental perspective may be helpful. For example, in order to understand fracture in late life one must consider inadequate peak bone mass early in life, accelerated bone loss due to menopause at midlife, and physical inactivity in later life (Riggs & Melton, 1988). The same is true of the life span development of health-promoting or health-damaging behaviors.

3. Older people are more likely to have multiple disorders and sensory deficits that may interact with the assessment and treatment process.

4. Not all physiological functions decline with age (Minaker & Rowe, 1985; Timiras, 1988). Not all age-related physiological changes result in disease (Whitbourne, 1985).

5. The older the organism, the longer it will take it to return to baseline given an equal stress. This appears to be true at the cellular and subcellular levels as well as in terms of complex behavioral functions such as lovemaking.

6. In contrast with early development, where knowledge of age provides developmental benchmarks, in later life, age itself contains

relatively less information. Distance from death, for example, may be a more informative variable for some behaviors (White & Cunningham, 1988).

Selections from the Knowledge Base

One way to illustrate concepts in developmental health psychology is to describe representative theoretical models and research programs that have been successful in linking traits or behavior to pathophysiological mechanisms or well-measured diseased groups of aging persons at different phases of the life cycle.

Theoretical Models

Theoretical models of aging rarely deal with health and diseases. Timiras's (1988) model of homeostasis, as seen in Figure 1, describes progressive stages of homeostasis from normal functioning to death in a health–disease framework. This model is consistent with a stress model. At basal levels, changes in most body systems are slight, and regulatory mechanisms compensate to preserve function. As stress increases, however, the limits of the compensatory processes are reached and breakdown occurs.

Although Timiras's model is useful for thinking about aging and health, it does not focus on the behavioral, psychophysiological, and environmental variables that are of specific interest to psychologists. Figure 2 presents a model we are using in our study of psychological precursors of coronary heart disease (Siegler, 1988; Williams, 1989). I use this model to illustrate how behavioral characteristics can be related to (a) biological, behavioral, and social risk factors for disease; (b) underlying disease mechanisms; and (c) specific definitions of coronary heart disease observed over a 5- to 10-year period. This model suggests that multiple measures of the psychological characteristics are in order and that genetic influences may be indexed by family history of coronary heart disease and hypertension. It supposes that factors in the social environment such as social and environmental supports, job strain, and smoking are mediated centrally and indexed by neuroendocrine and catecholamine indices, which then have an impact on target organs assessed by measures of blood pressure and blood lipids. These blood changes are presumed, over time, to be linked to coronary disease outcomes such as heart attacks, sudden death, and chest pain (angina pectoris). This model is testable and incorporates many of the behavioral risk factors discussed later in this chapter.

Configuration of the model in Figure 2 depends on research in the psychophysiology of aging. Psychophysiological theories of age-related

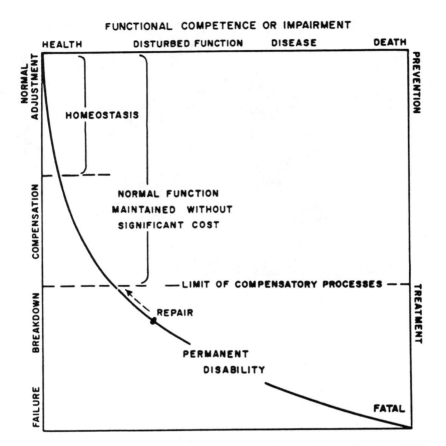

Figure 1. Timiras's model of homeostasis. Reprinted from Timiras (1988, p. 193) by permission.

declines in performance assume a U-shaped arousal function and general effects. Psychophysiological variables are involved in a number of the diseases common to later life. A first step in understanding their role in disease in old age is to examine age differences in the relation of these variables to performance when disease is not present.

A study by Jennings, Stiller, and Brock (1988) represents the contribution that theory-based cross-sectional studies can make. The researchers reasoned as follows: If older people's poor performance on laboratory tasks is explained by the fact that they are overaroused, then this should be evident in their cardiovascular physiology and neuroendocrine responses observed during a series of experiments using noise as a stressor. For young people, noise produced more errors and slower

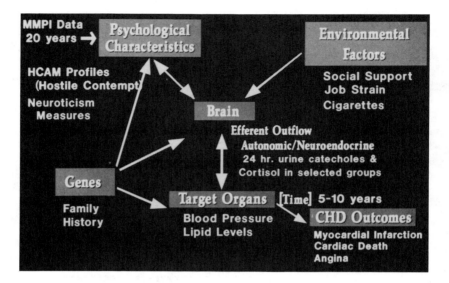

Figure 2. A model to test psychosocial factors in the health of coronary heart tissue.

times; for older people, noise also slowed reaction time, but it did not increase errors. Thus, the older participants were not as adversely affected by the noise. Older persons reported higher arousal, had vascular indices consistent with higher arousal, and had higher levels of some catecholamines. These differences were not consistent across phases of the task or the various indices of physiological and neuroendocrine reactivity. These researchers concluded that "the interplay of neuro-psychological, endocrine, and age-induced structural change suggests that a global concept such as general arousal will not be a useful concept for the psychophysiology of aging" (p. 278). They concluded furthermore that "the autonomic nervous system and neuroendocrine system respond differentially rather than as an arousal system" and that "aging may alter how autonomic and endocrine support is provided to ongoing processes" (p. 179). Thus, the underlying mechanisms are not simple, and their interactions with the aging process may well vary enormously.

The importance of such studies is that even the more specific model (Figure 2) depends implicitly on an underlying model of the psycho-physiology and neuroendocrinology of stress that must relate behavior to disease outcomes. The task ahead is to understand what is changing with aging and whether aging is the same in those persons who have specific diseases, compared with their peers without disease. These disease-specific approaches are important additions to the field. An example is the current explosion of research on Alzheimer's disease, which is expanding our knowledge of the neuropsychology of later life (e.g., Albert & Moss, 1989).

Research Paradigms

Three research programs that make particularly good use of longitudinal data represent the critical core of developmental health psychology. As Matthews (1988a) pointed out in her meta-analysis of the coronary heart disease and Type A behavior pattern, cross-sectional studies are "especially useful for generating hypotheses to be tested in later prospective (longitudinal) designs and for low frequency diseases" (p. 374). If data are obtained only at one point in time, however, "it is just as likely that the disease causes the behavior as that the psychological state causes the disease" (Matthews, 1988a, p. 374).

Building on data from the Baltimore Longitudinal Study of Aging (Costa, Fleg, McCrae, & Lakatta, 1982), Costa (1987) used longitudinal data from the National Health and Nutrition Examination Survey (NHANES) to explore the relations among neuroticism, chest pain, and coronary artery disease.

The NHANES involved a sample of 14,407 adults aged 24 and older who were examined and interviewed between April 1971 and October 1979. A subset ($n = 6,902$) had a physical examination and took the general well-being schedule—an 18-item scale of recent psychological function and well-being. At this initial examination, 1,911 persons reported chest pain, and the remainder did not. Those who reported chest pain had significantly higher neuroticism scores than those who did not. Measures of neuroticism may confound the assessment of a disorder such as angina pectoris, which depends on subjects' reports of chest pain. For example, in one study, those referred for coronary angiography who were found to be free of disease were also higher in measures of neuroticism (Elias & Robbins, 1987).

Costa (1987) compared the neuroticism scores of the 217 NHANES participants who died from myocardial infarction by follow-up 10 years later with the scores of the survivors ($n = 5,493$). He found no significant differences. That is, in the logistic regression equation predicting death from myocardial infarction, neuroticism was not a risk factor, although, as shown in Table 1, the other risk factors (age, sex, history of myocardial infarction, and chest pain) measured as expected.

This work illustrates the importance of longitudinal follow-up data with specific disease endpoints. Furthermore, the size and scope of the study mean that sufficient events were observed in a 10-year period.

Another example is provided by Schaie's (1983; in press) ongoing study of intelligence across the adult life span. To explain observed pattern of stability and decline in intelligence, he examined incidents of disease in a sample of 109 individuals over age 50, some with stable and

Table 1
Relative Risk for Myocardial Infarction Death (n = 217) Versus Survival (n = 5,493) at Follow-Up in Total Sample (NHANES)

Predictor at Time 1	Relative Risk	p
Age (> 60)	4.6	.000
Sex (men)	2.8	.000
History of myocardial infarction	3.7	.000
Cholesterol (> 250)	1.5	.013
Systolic blood pressure (> 140)	2.5	.000
Smoking (> 100 cigarettes)	—	.088
Chest pain or discomfort	1.5	.019
Neuroticism	—	.258

Note. From "Influences of the Normal Personality Dimension of Neuroticism on Chest Pain Symptoms and Coronary Artery Disease" by P. T. Costa, Jr., 1987, American Journal of Cardiology, 60, p. 23J. Reprinted by permission.

some with declining patterns of intellectual performance. Medical histories for the 7-year period prior to evaluation were examined, and all diseases and illness episodes were noted. The two groups were not different on variables that indexed total numbers of incidents or episodes of illness. When incidents and episodes were restricted to heart disease and hypertension, however, significant differences emerged. Those who declined had, on average, twice as many cardiovascular-system-related medical visits and 1.5 times as many cardiovascular illness incidents as did those who had stable patterns of intellectual test scores. Incidents of hospitalization for cardiovascular disease were 10 times more likely for those who declined. Thus, although general health may not be related to patterns of intellectual decline with age, a particular type of illness (e.g., cardiovascular disease) may be.

A different approach is represented in the work of M. F. Elias and his colleagues, who have conducted a 10-year longitudinal study of a hypertensive group and a matched normotensive group initially aged 40 to 58 (Elias, Schultz, Robbins, & Elias, 1989). Consistent small differences in intellectual and neuropsychological performance were observed in those with hypertension. These differences were small enough to have no practical significance in the age range studied. (Schultz, Elias, Robbins, Streeten, & Blakemore, 1986). When studied longitudinally, the impact of the disease was shown to be modest. This may be due to individuals' ability to adapt to the disease or to selection factors where the most impaired participants are less likely to continue in the study.

Thus, in the first paradigm described (Costa, 1987), the research approach was an attempt to relate preexisting behavioral risk factors to health outcome. In Schaie's study, incidents of ill health were related to long-term behavioral outcomes in stability and to change in cognitive functions, whereas the behavior of those with and without a chronic disease were compared longitudinally in the work by Elias and his colleagues.

Moderating Variables in Developmental Health Psychology

Human beings are sick or healthy as individuals but also as people living in social systems. Only 5% are in nursing homes; thus, the vast majority remain in the community, often near family and longtime friends.

We place great emphasis on the role of social support in helping people to cope with disease in later life. In addition, epidemiologic data indicate that social support is health-protective; individuals without extensive social support are at greater risk for disease (e.g., Cohen, 1988; House, Landis, & Umberson, 1988). We do not yet know how and why this is true, although a number of researchers are trying to find explanations. Whatever mechanisms operate, they probably do not vary as a function of age (Siegler & Poon, 1989). Thus, just as a family systems approach is often appropriate in the treatment of younger individuals, it is similarly appropriate in work with older adults.

Felton and Revenson (in press) review the social and psychological factors in developmental health psychology with an emphasis on factors related to illness onset, experience of illness, course of recovery of chronic illnesses, architecture of episodes, and prevention. This work has direct clinical implications for those working with the elderly because it emphasizes the ways that age may interact with illness and provides a scientific base for developing clinical intervention strategies targeted to the older person's health behaviors.

Another growing body of literature (see Baltes & Baltes, 1986) relates control processes to health in later life. This research is based on the premise that in later life, both environmental and biological events lead to decreases in actual and perceived control (Rodin, 1986). Rodin and Timko (in press) point out the need to evaluate both the environments where control enhancements have been successful and also the possible behavioral physiological and stress-related mechanisms that may mediate such effects. They also suggest there may be differences in preference for control and that the need for control, or lack thereof, may have negative effects on health outcomes.

Dealing With Risk

We as a society are overwhelmed with conflicting advice about modifying our behavior on the basis of epidemiologic studies of various diseases. The morning news programs tell us to take an aspirin a day to prevent heart disease but to watch out for stroke. Drink one drink a day to reduce heart disease, but be prepared for an increased probability of breast cancer. Translating results from group data into individual predictions is not simple in psychology, nor is it in epidemiology. These recommendations depend on an understanding of the concept of relative risk. Relative risk is a ratio of the incidence of a particular disease in those persons who have the risk factors, compared with disease incidence in those persons without the factors (Fletcher, Fletcher, & Wagner, 1982). Because disease is often multifactorial, these risk estimates are calculated with logistic regression models so that the relations among risk factors can be considered simultaneously when predicting a dichotomous (disease–no disease) outcome (Kleinbaum, Kupper, & Morganstern, 1982).

Definition of Risk and Biological Risk Factors

What is a risk factor? It is a characteristic that increases the probability that a person will develop a disease. Risk factors can be biological or behavioral.

Prominent among the biological risk factors are age, sex, and family history (as an index of genetic variation). Most diseases have different distributions by age and sex. The understanding of why age and sex are risk factors is a critical one. Of the diseases discussed in Table 2, all tend to increase with age and most have age-by-sex interactions. For example, coronary heart disease increases in incidence about 10 to 15 years later for women than for men (Johansson, Vedin, & Wilhelmsson, 1983).

Menopause produces changes related to metabolic (changes in estrogen) and autonomic nervous system imbalances (such as hot flushes). Prevalence estimates for any particular symptom, however, are close to 30%, and most can be treated medically. Menopause does not appear to cause poorer health or to increase use of medical services (McKinlay, McKinlay, & Brambilla, 1987). Some excellent self-help manuals have appeared (Doress & Siegal, 1987). "Clearly, the psychosocial aspects of menopause are more linked to the social and cultural climate than to internal biopsychological and physiological change" (Markson, 1987, p. 438). The physiological implications of menopause, however, may have important psychological components (Matthews, 1986).

After menopause (around age 50), women appear to catch up with men in incidence of coronary heart disease. The largest sex-factor difference in later life is in survival. The reason for this is still not well understood. Recent work suggests that there may be important sex-factor differences in cardiovascular reactivity that produce less coronary heart disease in women (Matthews & Stoney, 1988). Verbrugge (1985) suggests that part of the difference in survival rates may be related to differences in risk-factor profiles for major diseases such as smoking. The data

Table 2
Behavioral Risk Factors

Risk Factor	Symptom/Disease	Reference
Smoking	Bone loss/osteoporosis	Riggs & Melton (1988)
	Coronary heart disease (CHD)	Dawber (1980)
	Myocardial infarction/sudden death	Ostfeld (1986)
	In elderly: death	Kannel & Vokonas (1986)
	Cancer of lung, mouth, larynx, bladder	Marshall & Graham (1986)
	Emphysema	
Alcohol	Cancer of stomach, breast	Kasl (1986)
	Falls	Mossey (1985)
Obesity	Hypertension, Diabetes Mellitus	Ostfeld (1986)
High lipids	CHD	Cooper (1988)
High fat/Low fiber	Cancer of colon, rectum, breast, prostrate	Marshall & Graham (1986)
Hypertension	CHD	Kannel & Vokonas (1986)
Diabetes	CHD	
Type A behavior	CHD	Matthews (1988a)
Hostility	CHD	Williams (1989)
Job strain	CHD	Karasek et al. (1988)
Sexual behavior	AIDS, cervical cancer	Marshall & Graham (1986)

indicate that current cohorts of women are smoking more (McGinnis, Shopland, & Brown, 1987).

Menopause also produces accelerated bone loss that leads to increased risk for osteoporosis and fracture later in life (Riggs & Melton, 1988). Although men do not have a change in sexual function equivalent to menopause, there is an increase in male sexual dysfunction with age that is largely a result of associated diseases (Herman, 1987).

Health-Damaging Behavior

As shown in Table 2, the major behavioral risk factors for some of the diseases of most concern to developmental health psychologists are smoking, alcohol use, obesity, cholesterol level, Type A behavior pattern, hostility, job strain, psychosocial stress, and sexual behavior. Some risk factors are not specific to one disease. In general these factors have been shown to have effects even after statistically controlling for age and sex.

A literature is developing about the best techniques for health promotion and disease prevention. Data from studies such as the Framingham Study, which started in 1949 with 5,029 men and women aged 30 to 62 at time of entry, indicate that modification of risk factors during later life are worth the effort. Kannel and Vokonas (1986) found that, although coronary heart disease increases with age even in persons with low levels of known risk factors, age-matched peers at high levels of risk have even more disease. Risk profiles that predicted premature coronary heart disease also predicted it among elderly adults in the Framingham Study.

Preventive Behaviors

Table 3 shows some of the major preventive behaviors (factors that reduce risk). These include diet to reduce fat and increase fiber consumption, exercise, use of aspirin, internal control, social support, good health habits, and regular medical care (Schoenbach, 1985).

Because of their expertise in understanding and modifying behavior, psychologists have major contributions to make in helping older people

Table 3
Preventive Behaviors

Preventive Behavior	Effect on Symptom/Disease	Reference
Diet: Vitamin D Diet: Calcium supplement	Reduce bone loss	Riggs & Melton (1988)
Exercise	Reduce bone loss Reduce heart disease mortality	Riggs & Melton (1988) Paffenbarger, Hyde, Albin, & Hsieh (1986)
Aspirin	Reduce heart disease	Steering Committee of the Physicians' Health Study Research Group (1988)
Fat reduction	Reduce heart disease	Ostfeld (1986)
Social support	Reduce mortality	Berkman (1985)
Internal control	Increase self-care	Rodin & Timko (in press)

implement these behavior changes. Psychologists have a role to play also in the treatment of the diseases of later life. For example, behavioral treatment principles have been found to be effective in the management of pain in patients with osteoarthritis (Keefe, Caldwell, Queen, Gil, Martinez, Crisson, Ogden, & Nunley, 1987) and a variety of types of chronic pain (Puder, 1988). Behavior modification (M. M. Baltes, 1987) and biofeedback (Morrell, 1987) are of proven value for older patients. In institutional settings, manipulation of actual as well as perceived control has improved patient outcomes (Rodin, 1986).

Methodological Issues

Developmental health psychology has progressed to the point where we have many methodological issues to confront. Several are discussed briefly here. These issues are important because they influence the conclusions we draw from our research and the effectiveness of our attempts to translate these conclusions into practice.

Age as a Variable

In order to understand the three-way interaction of health, behavior, and age, it is necessary to include age in the research design and to analyze the data for its effect. This seems obvious. Yet a review of the published research on four major diseases of concern in later life in seven major behavioral medicine journals between 1982 and 1985 revealed otherwise (Morrell, Hoelscher, Anderson, & Jordan, 1988). Elderly adults were underutilized in these studies compared with their prevalence as patients. More troublesome is the fact that only about a quarter of the studies related age to outcome measures, whereas up to three fourths controlled for age either in the design by matching or in the analyses.

Chronological age, however, may not be the most important age to consider in a study. It may be more important to consider the age of the disease. For example, Buck, Baker, Bass, and Donner (1987) examined hypertension as a risk factor in a sample of older adults. They found that excess risk declined sharply for those diagnosed as hypertensive in later life (age 60 to 65) compared with those whose hypertension was "older" (i.e., earlier in onset). The excess risk was only 1.2 for those with "young" hypertension. Thus, there may well be multiple ages to be considered. Age-matched control groups are critical for cross-sectional studies in developmental health psychology.

Selection of Control Groups

What are the appropriate characteristics of those individuals who will form the control group in the study of a disease in later life? For example, should they have another disease to control for illness behaviors? Should those in the control group have a variety of other diseases, or should they all have the same disease? Must the control group be of the same sex? Should they have comparable educational or socioeconomic backgrounds? Is it appropriate to use individuals as controls who merely have not been diagnosed as having the disease? As described earlier, Lakatta (1987) showed that differing criteria for the definition of heart disease produced different samples of control subjects.

The results of studies of hypertension (Elias, Robbins, & Schulz, 1987) and chronic obstructive pulmonary disease (Dye, 1988) indicate that the largest effects of disease will be observed when comparisons are made of those with verified disease and those who are healthy. Comparisons with other age-matched patient groups will produce smaller effects. Thus, the conclusions we draw about the relation between a disease and behavior as a function of age may depend, in large part, on the control groups used.

Measurement of Disease and Health

We must be concerned about the measurement of health and disease separately. Health is usually defined by exclusion of various diseases. We use self-ratings, physician ratings, and performance–fitness criteria. Measurement of disease is different and depends on diagnostic accuracy, symptom reporting, technological sophistication in an area, and the assessment of status from archive sources such as death certificates and hospital records. Definitions of diseases and their meaning change over time. Pryor et al. (1987) reviewed the enhanced survival of patients with coronary heart disease. They found that as new treatments develop and succeed, we are predicting different outcomes.

Each body system and each disease will have a set of indices that are used for diagnosis and rating of severity of the disease. It is important that these procedures be understood and that the indices be used properly. It is also important to know the reliability of a particular measurement and the conditions under which it was taken, as well as the extent to which disease ascertainment is confused with treatment strategy. Such specific requirements make studies of psychological factors in "disease" suspect, as one cannot postulate a potential mechanism for understanding a multiplicity of processes. Matthews (1988a), in her critique of Type A meta-analyses, indicates some of the details about coronary heart disease that a psychologist must have in order to fully understand the literature.

Many medical diagnostic procedures obtain an index of a physiological function and compare it with a criterion to determine if the physiological function is within normal range; if it is not, health is questioned. One problem with such measures is that the normal range may be age-dependent. Because such precise indices of physiological function often require testing that is invasive and expensive, it is difficult to justify testing large numbers of control subjects to determine age-corrected criteria for health.

Furthermore, it is often difficult to determine the best physiological index for a particular disease. In a series of studies summarized by a study by Elias and Robbins (1987), three measures of coronary artery disease severity were assessed by cardiologists who evaluated 19 coronary artery segments. Six dependent variables were constructed. Elias and Robbins found that the six variables were positively correlated (ranging from .42 to .97), but the measures had differential correlations with age and education, as well as with the behavioral measures used in their study. Thus, not all physiological indices behave the same. A full understanding of exactly what they measure is critical.

Self-rated health is an important index of functioning and even of longevity (Mossey & Shapiro, 1982). It is related to the degree of impairment a person has from various causes and to physicians' ratings of an individual's competence. It is, however, a summary measure that involves both physical and mental health.

Health ratings by physicians often are not simple, either. Consider, for example, the physician rating scale based on physical examinations used by Peterson, Seligman, and Vaillant (1988); this scale is shown in Table 4 on the left side. Diagnostic categories, severity of illness, functional ability, and survivorship are all combined into a single scale that has strange psychometric properties, yet captures what might be a common-sense way to divide health into five levels, where death is the final status. Functional capacity of individuals rated 2, 3, or 4, however, cannot be assumed to be similarly ordered.

A different approach is to focus on function rather than health, as shown on the right side of Table 4. This scale was developed by Nowlin to code self-reports of disease, functional limitations, current medications, and functional ability in a self-report mail questionnaire (Hooker, Siegler, & Nowlin, 1988).

Each approach can be useful. The choice depends on the research question and the age of the persons being tested. The ratings on the left in Table 4 are more appropriate for a younger, and thus generally healthier, group, whereas the system on the right is more likely to be appropriate for an elderly group of respondents.

Death certificates give information on the cause of death. Thus, if the cause of death is known, then it can be used to classify the deceased person with survivors who have the sample pathology (e.g., sudden death from heart attack with other evidence of myocardial infarction), as

Table 4
Examples of Physical Health Scales in the Literature

Scale used in serial physical exams performed by personal physicians and rated by research internist. A rating was done for each age period: 25, 30, 35, 40, 45, 50, 55, and 60. (Peterson, Seligman, & Vaillant, 1988, p. 24.)	Rating scale made by physician who had examined respondents in 1969, 1970, 1972, and 1974 on the basis of self-report of diseases, medications, and hospitalizations, in a mail questionnaire in 1984 and again in 1986 (from Hooker, Siegler, & Nowlin, 1988).
1 = Good health; normal	0 = Normal; no evidence of disease
2 = Multiple minor complaints: mild back trouble, prostatitis, gout, kidney stones, single joint problems, chronic ear problems, and so on	1 = Minor symptoms or signs of disease
3 = Probably irreversible chronic illness without disability; illness that will not fully remit and will probably progress— for example, treated hypertension, emphysema with cor pulmonale, and diabetes	2 = Normal activity with some effort; some signs of disease
4 = Probably irreversible chronic illness with disability—for example, myocardial infarction with angina, disabling back trouble, hypertension and extreme obesity, diabetes and severe arthritis, and multiple sclerosis	3 = Unable to work; able to care for self
5 = Dead	4 = Able to care for most needs but requires occasional assistance
	5 = Requires considerable assistance and frequent medical care
	6 = Unable to care for self; requires equivalent of institution or hospital care

opposed to all-cause mortality. These are very different outcome variables. In the first case, the intent of the research is to understand what behavioral factors may be involved in prediction of a particular pathological status. With all-cause mortality or length of survivorship, the emphasis is on the overall homeostatic response of the organism.

Symptom checklists are another common self-report technique. They are just that—symptoms. Costa and McCrae (1987) argued convincingly that, without validating information, one cannot know the extent to which symptom reports reflect levels of the personality portion of neuroticism scales related to somatic complaints, rather than evidence of a particular disorder. Self-reports of drug use, medical and surgical visits, and limitations of activity are also important data that can be used to estimate health. We do not know, however, how accurate such self-reports are. Sackett (1979) reviewed various sources of bias. Phrasing of the questions probably has major influences on the quality of the information. The socioeconomic status of the respondents may also affect the amount of information known and how questions are interpreted. Income is related to access to health care. For example, diseases such as hypertension are asymptomatic; unless blood pressure is measured as part of an examination, the disease is not discovered. A very cooperative and willing subject cannot report information that he or she does not have. Similarly, disease may be detected later, even when symptoms are present. Data from sources such as the National Health Interview Survey provide some models about how such questions are asked. It is important to develop strategies to validate all self-report measures (Bergner & Rothman, 1987) in order to know how to interpret them.

Implications

What are the future directions for developmental health psychology as a scientific area and as background for a practice specialty?

It is probably no longer helpful to study only health versus disease. These constructs are difficult to use in research. On the other hand, we can study the behavioral factors in a specific disease, or we can model the real world and study combinations of diseases that are observed.

In the past we have traded internal validity for external validity. We have used excellent behavioral measures on relatively small, intensively studied samples that are not representative. We have not included important behavioral variables in national data bases. We must design behavioral measures that can be used with representative samples.

The age span of valid interest to us is approaching 100 years. We need to develop models to study those who are surviving to such ages to add to our present work, which focuses on mortality and those who do not survive.

We need to integrate the theoretical perspectives from life span developmental psychology (P. B. Baltes, 1987; Nesselroade, 1988), psychophysiology, and behavioral medicine to form the theoretical underpinnings of developmental health psychology. It is not sufficient to consider the older person who comes to the developmental health psychologist for assistance from only one of these perspectives. If one does so, important variables may be ignored.

Our role as psychologists does not end with the development of the knowledge base. We know data relating personality to disease are often misinterpreted to blame the victim for the disease. Our data in these areas will be used by others to make policy, whether we like it or not. Others using our data may not use our value systems either. We must be involved in the public debate; it is our responsibility to participate. We must make sure that our findings about the three-way interaction of behavior, health, and age are interpreted properly.

References

Albert, M. S. (1989). Assessment of cognitive dysfunction. In M. S. Albert & M. B. Moss (Eds.), *Geriatric neuropsychology* (pp. 57–81). New York: Guilford Press.

Albert, M.S., & Moss, M. B. (1989). *Geriatric neuropsychology*. New York: Guilford Press.

Baltes, M. M. (1987). Behavior modification. In G. L. Maddox, R. Atchley, L. W. Poon, G. Roth, I. C. Siegler, R. Steinberg, & R. Corsini (Eds.), *Encyclopedia of aging*. New York: Springer.

Baltes, M. M., & Baltes, P. B. (Eds.). (1986). *The psychology of control*. Hillsdale, NJ: Lawrence Erlbaum.

Baltes, P. B. (1987). Theoretical propositions on life-span developmental psychology: On the dynamics between growth and decline. *Developmental Psychology, 23*, 611–626.

Bergner, M., & Rothman, M. L. (1987). Health status measures: An overview and guide for selection. In L. Breslow, J. E. Fielding, & L. B. Lave (Eds.), *Annual review of public health, 8*, 191–210.

Berkman, L. F. (1985). The relationship of social networks and social support to morbidity and mortality. In S. Cohen & S. L. Syme (Eds.), *Social support and health* (pp. 241–262). New York: Academic Press.

Brody, J. A., Brock, D. B., & Williams, T. F. (1987). Trends in the health of the elderly population. In L. Breslow, J. E. Fielding, & L. B. Lave (Eds.), *Annual review of public health, 8*, 211–234.

Buck, C., Baker, P., Bass, M., & Donner, A. (1987). The prognosis of hypertension according to age at onset. *Hypertension, 9*, 204–208.

Cohen, S. (1988). Psychosocial models of the role of social support in the etiology of physical disease. *Health Psychology, 7*, 269–297.

Cooper, K. H. (1988). *Controlling cholesterol*. New York: Bantam Books.

Costa, P. T., Jr. (1987). Influence of the normal personality dimension of neuroticism on chest pain symptoms and coronary artery disease. *American Journal of Cardiology, 60*, 20J–26J.

Costa, P. T., Jr., Fleg, J. L., McCrae, R. R., & Lakatta, E. G. (1982). Neuroticism, coronary artery disease and chest pain complaints: Cross-sectional longitudinal studies. *Experimental Aging Research*, 37–44.

Costa, P. T., Jr., & McCrae, R. R. (1987). Neuroticism, somatic complaints and disease: Is the bark worse than the bite? *Journal of Personality, 55*, 299–316.

Dawber, T. R. (1980). *The Framingham Study: The epidemiology of atherosclerotic disease*. Cambridge: Harvard University Press.

Doress, P. B., & Siegal, D. L. (1987). *Ourselves, growing older*. New York: Simon and Schuster.

Dye, C. J. (1988). *Psychological adjustment to chronic illness: Age and disease effects.* Unpublished manuscript.

Eisdorfer, C., & Wilkie, F. E. (1977). Stress, disease, aging, and behavior. In J. E. Birren & K. W. Schaie (Eds.), *Handbook of the psychology of aging* (pp. 251–275). New York: Van Nostrand Reinhold.

Elias, M. F., Elias, J. W., & Elias, P. K. (in press). Biological and health influences. In J. E. Birren & K. W. Schaie (Eds.), *Handbook of the psychology of aging* (3rd ed.).

Elias, M. F., & Robbins, M. A. (1987). Use of cinearteriography in behavioral studies of patients with chest pain in the absence of clinically significant coronary artery disease. In J. W. Elias & P. H. Marshall (Eds.), *Cardiovascular disease and behavior* (p. 106). Washington, DC: Hemisphere.

Elias, M. F., Robbins, M. A., & Schulz, N. (1987). Influence of hypertension on intellectual performance: Causation or speculation? In J. W. Elias & P. H. Marshall (Eds.), *Cardiovascular disease and behavior* (pp. 107–149). Washington, DC: Hemisphere.

Elias, M. F., Schultz, N. R., Robbins, M. A., & Elias, P. K. (1989). A longitudinal study of neuropsychological performance by hypertensives and normotensives: A third measurement point. *Journal of Gerontology: Psychological Science, 44*, P25–P28.

Felton, B. J., & Revenson, T. A. (in press). The psychology of health: Issues in the field with special focus on the older person. In I. A. Parham, L. W. Poon, & I. C. Siegler (Eds.), *Aging curriculum content for education in the social/behavioral sciences.* New York: Springer.

Fletcher, R. H., Fletcher, S. W., & Wagner, E. H. (1982). *Clinical epidemiology—the essentials.* Baltimore: Williams & Wilkins.

Herman, S. (1987). Initial assessment of men with sexual complaints: The male sexual dysfunction protocol. In J. A. Blumenthal & D. C. McKee (Eds.), *Applications in behavioral medicine and health psychology: A clinician's sourcebook* (pp. 115–123). Sarasota, FL: Professional Research Exchange.

Hooker, K., Seigler, I. C., & Nowlin, J. B. (1988, August). *Personality and health: Data from the Duke second longitudinal study.* Paper presented at the convention of the American Psychological Association, Atlanta, GA.

House, J. S., Landis, K. R., & Umberson, D. (1988). Social relationships and health. *Science, 241*, 540–545.

Jennings, J. R., Stiller, R., & Brock, K. (1988). Are changes in performance with noise and age due to adrenergic arousal? *Psychobiology, 16*(3), 270–280.

Johansson, S., Vedin, A., & Wilhelmsson, C. (1983). Myocardial infarction in women. *Epidemiologic Reviews, 5*, 67–95.

Jones, H. B. (1959). The relation of human health to age, place, and time. In J. E. Birren (Ed.), *Handbook of aging and the individual.* Chicago: University of Chicago Press. (pp. 336–363).

Kannel, W. B., & Vokonas, P. S. (1986). Primary risk factors for coronary heart disease in the elderly: The Framingham Study. In N. K. Wegner, C. D. Furtberg, & E. Pitt (Eds.), *Coronary heart disease in the elderly* (pp. 60–93). New York: Elsevier Scientific.

Karasek, R. A., Theorell, T., Schwartz, J. E., Schanall, P. L., Peiper, C. F., & Michella, J. L. (1988). Job characteristics in relation to the prevalence of myocardial infarction in the U.S. Health Examination Survey (HES) and the Health and

Nutrition Examination Survey (NHANES). *American Journal of Public Health, 78*, 910–918.

Kasl, S. V. (1986). The detection and modification of psychosocial and behavioral risk factors. In L. H. Aiken, & D. Mechanic (Eds.), *Applications of social science to clinical medicine and health policy* (pp. 359–391). New Brunswick, NJ: Rutgers University Press.

Keefe, F. J., Caldwell, D. S., Queen, K., Gil, K. M., Martinez, S., Crisson, J. E., Ogden, W., & Nunley, J. (1987). Osteoarthritic knee pain: A behavioral analysis. *Pain, 28*, 309–321.

Kleinbaum, D., Kupper, L., & Morganstern, H. (1982). *Epidemiologic research.* New York: Van Nostrand Reinhold.

Lakatta, E. G. (1987). The aging heart: Myth and realities. In J. W. Elias & P. H. Marshall (Eds.), *Cardiovascular disease and behavior* (pp. 179–193). Washington, DC: Hemisphere.

Markson, E. W. (1987). Menopause: psychosocial aspects. In G. L. Maddox et al. (Eds.), *Encyclopedia of aging* (pp. 437–439). New York: Springer.

Marshall, J., & Graham, S. (1986). Cancer. In L. H. Aiken & D. Mechanic (Eds.), *Applications of social science to clinical medicine and health policy* (pp. 157–173). New Brunswick, NJ: Rutgers University Press.

Matthews, K. A. (1988a). Coronary heart disease and Type A behaviors: Update as an alternate to the Booth–Kewley and Friedman (1987) quantitative review. *Psychological Bulletin, 104*, 373–380.

Matthews, K. A. (1988b, August). Behavioral antecedents of coronary heart disease. Division 38 Presidential Address presented at the convention of the American Psychological Association, Atlanta, GA.

Matthew, K. A., & Stoney, C. M. (1988). Influence of age and sex on cardiovascular responses during stress. *Psychosomatic Medicine, 50*, 46–56.

McGinnis, J. M., Shopland, D., & Brown, C. (1987). Tobacco and health: Trends in smoking and smokeless tobacco consumption in the United States. In L. Breslow, J. E. Fielding, & L. B. Lave (Eds.), *Annual Review of Public Health, 8*, pp. 441–468.

McKinlay, J. B., McKinlay, S. M., & Brambilla, D. J. (1987). Health status and utilization behavior associated with menopause. *American Journal of Epidemiology, 125*(1), 110–121.

Minaker, K. L., & Rowe, J. W. (1985). Health and disease among the oldest old: A clinical perspective. *Milbank Memorial Fund Quarterly: Health and Society, 63*, 324–349.

Morrell, E. M. (1987). Biofeedback. In G. L. Maddox et al. (Eds.), *Encyclopedia of aging.* New York: Springer.

Morrell, E. M., Hoelscher, T. J., Anderson, N. B., & Jordan, J. S. (1988, April). *The aging variable in behavioral medicine journals.* Paper presented at the meetings of the Society of Behavioral Medicine, Boston, MA.

Mossey, J. M. (1985). Social and psychological factors related to falls among the elderly. *Clinics in Geriatric Medicine, 1*(3), 541–552.

Mossey, J. M., & Shapiro, E. (1982). Self-rated health: A predictor of mortality among the elderly. *American Journal of Public Health, 7*(8), 800–808.

Nesselroade, J. R. (1988, August), *The warp and woof of development's fabric.* Division 20 invited address presented at the convention of the American Psychological Association, Atlanta, GA.

Okun, M. A., & Stock, W. A. (1987). Correlates and components of subjective well-being in the elderly. *Journal of Applied Gerontology, 6*, 95–112.

Ostfeld, A. M. (1986). Cardiovascular disease. In L. H. Aiken & D. Mechanic (Eds.), *Applications of social science to clinical medicine and health policy* (pp. 129–155). New Brunswick, NJ: Rutgers University Press.

Paffenbarger, R. S., Hyde, R. T., Albin, L. W., & Hsieh, C. C. (1986). Physical activity, all-cause mortality, and longevity of college alumni. *The New England Journal of Medicine, 314*(10), 605–613.

Pearlman, R. A., & Uhlmann, R. F. (1988). Quality of life in chronic disease: Perceptions of elderly patients. *Journal of Gerontology: Medical Sciences, 43*(2), M25–M30.

Peterson, C., Seligman, M. E. P., & Vaillant, G. E. (1988). Pessimistic explanatory style is a risk factor for physical illness. *Journal of Personality and Social Psychology, 55*(1), 23–27.

Pryor, D. B., Harrell, F. E., Rankin, J. S., Lee, K. L., Mulbaier, L. H., Oldham, H. N., Hlatky, M. A., Mark, D. B., Reves, J. G., & Califf, R. M. (1987). The changing survival benefits of coronary revascularization over time. *Circulation, 76 (suppl. V)*, V13–V21.

Puder, R. S. (1988). Age analysis of cognitive-behavioral group therapy for chronic pain outpatients. *Psychology and Aging, 3*(2), 204–207.

Riggs, B. L., & Melton, L. J., III (1988). Osteoporosis and age-related fracture syndromes. In D. Evered & J. Whelan (Eds.), *Research and the aging population* (pp. 129–142). Chichester, U.K.: John Wiley & Sons, Ltd.

Rodin, J. (1986). Aging and health: Effects of the sense of control. *Science, 233*, 1271–1276.

Rodin, J., & Timko, C. (in press). Sense of control, aging, and health. In M. Ory & R. Abeles (Eds.), *Aging, health, and behavior*. Baltimore: Johns Hopkins University Press.

Rosow, I. (1978). What is a cohort and why? *Human Development, 21*, 65–75.

Rowe, J. W., & Kahn, R. L. (1987). Human aging: Usual and successful. *Science, 237*, 143–149.

Sackett, D. L. (1979). Bias in analytic research. *Journal of Chronic Disease, 32*, 51–53.

Schaie, K. W. (1983). The Seattle Longitudinal Study: A 21-year exploration of psychometric intelligence in adulthood. In K. W. Schaie (Ed.), *Longitudinal studies of adult psychological development* (pp. 64–135). New York: Guilford Press.

Schaie, K. W. (in press). The optimization of cognitive functioning in old age: Predictions based on cohort-sequential and longitudinal data. In P. B. Baltes & M. M. Baltes (Eds.), *Longitudinal research and the study of successful (optimal) aging*. London: Cambridge University Press.

Schoenbach, V. J. (1985). Behavior and lifestyle as determinants of health and well-being in the elderly. In H. T. Phillips & S. A. Gaylord (Eds.), *Aging and public health* (pp. 183–216). New York: Springer.

Schultz, N. R., Elias, M. F., Robbins, M. A., Streeten, D. H. P., & Blakemore, N. (1986). A longitudinal comparison of hypertensives and normotensives on the Wechsler Adult Intelligence Scale: Initial findings. *Journal of Gerontology, 41*, 169–175.

Siegler, I. C. (1988). *Threats of internal validity in a prospective study of psychoso-*

cial precursors of CHD and CHD risk. Unpublished master's thesis. School of Public Health, University of North Carolina, Chapel Hill, NC.

Siegler, I. C., & Costa, P. I., Jr. (1985). Health behavior relationships. In J. E. Birren & K. W. Schaie (Eds.), *Handbook of the psychology of aging* (2nd ed.) (pp. 144–166). New York: Van Nostrand Reinhold.

Siegler, I. C., & Poon, L. W. (1989). The psychology of aging. In E. W. Busse & D. G. Blazer (Eds.), *Geriatric psychiatry* (pp. 163–201). Washington, DC: American Psychiatric Press.

The Steering Committee of the Physicians' Health Study Research Group. (1988). Preliminary report: Findings from the aspirin component of the ongoing physicians' health study. *The New England Journal of Medicine, 318*(4), 262–264.

Storandt, M. (1983), *Counseling and therapy with older adults*. Boston: Little, Brown.

Timiras, P. S. (1988). *Physiological basis of geriatrics*. New York: Macmillan.

Verbrugge, L. M. (1985). Gender and health: An update on the evidence. *Journal of Health and Social Behavior, 26* 156–182.

Welford, A. T., & Birren, J. E. (Eds.) (1965). *Aging behavior and the nervous system*. Springfield, IL: Charles C. Thomas.

Whitbourne, S. K. (1985). *The aging body*. New York: Springer-Verlag.

White, N., & Cunningham, W. R. (1988). Is terminal drop pervasive or specific? *Journal of Gerontology: Psychological Sciences, 43*, P141–P144.

Williams, R. B., Jr. (1989). *The trusting heart: Great news about Type A behavior*. New York: Times Books.

POLICY ISSUES IN AN AGING SOCIETY

B ernice L. Neugarten, Rothschild Distinguished Scholar at the University of Chicago's Center on Aging, Health, and Society, is a behavioral scientist specializing in adult development and aging. She has received many honors for her research and teaching, including: the Kleemeier Award from the Gerontological Society of America in 1971 for outstanding contributions to research in aging; the National Teaching Award from the American Psychological Foundation in 1975; the Distinguished Psychologist Award from the Illinois Psychological Association in 1979; the Distinguished Scientific Contribution Award of Division 20 of the American Psychological Association in 1980; an honorary Doctor of Science from the University of Southern California in 1980; and an honorary doctorate from the University of Nijmegen, the Netherlands, in 1988. In 1982 she was given the prestigious Brookdale Award from the Gerontological Society of America for outstanding contributions to gerontology, and in 1987 she was awarded the Sandoz International Prize for Research in gerontology. She is a fellow of the American Academy of Arts and Sciences and a senior member of the Institute of Medicine of the National Academy of Sciences. She has served as a member of the National Academy of Sciences Committee on the Aging Society.

Neugarten, formerly professor of human development at the University of Chicago, directed the Graduate Training Program in Adult Development and Aging there from 1958 to 1980. She was chairman of the

Committee on Human Development from 1969 to 1973 and the first chairman of the Committee on University Women during 1969–1970.

She has written or edited eight books and some 150 research papers, monographs, and review articles dealing with adult development, middle age and aging, the relations between age groups, and social policy issues. Among the books are *Society and Education, Personality in Middle and Late Life, Middle Age and Aging, Adjustment to Retirement, Social Status in the City, Social Policy, Social Ethics, and the Aging Society*, and *Age or Need? Public Policies for Older People.*

Neugarten has been active in numerous professional organizations and in public service. She has served as president of the Gerontological Society of America and as consultant for several years to the National Institute of Child Health and Human Development. She was a member of the Council of Representatives of the American Psychological Association, the Technical Committee on Research and Demonstration for the 1971 White House Conference on Aging, the Governing Council of the International Association of Gerontology, the National Advisory Council of the National Institute on Aging, and the Federal Council on the Aging. She served for a year as deputy chairperson for the 1981 White House Conference on Aging, then continued as a member of the National Advisory Committee and chairman of the Committee on Educational and Training Opportunities.

She has been an associate editor of the *Journal of Gerontology* and of *Human Development* and consulting editor to several other research journals.

Neugarten was born in Norfolk, Nebraska. She received a PhD from the Committee on Human Development at the University of Chicago.

POLICY ISSUES IN AN AGING SOCIETY

Introduction

In keeping with the broad title of this chapter, the issues we will discuss here are broad ones. The chapter is addressed to psychologists, primarily in their role as informed citizens in a rapidly changing society. At the same time, because the societal context shapes the nature of work, there are also implications for psychologists in their roles as academics and professionals.

The first part of the chapter deals with the changing age distribution of the American population and defines the term *the aging society*. In this context, it is unfortunate that social scientists and policymakers have for the most part focused attention upon only one segment of the population—those persons who have lived beyond their 65th birthday. Not only is age 65 becoming a less useful marker of old age than it was in earlier decades, but attention needs to be given also to the ways in which the presence of increasing numbers of older persons is changing all our social institutions and changing the lives of all persons, whether young, middle-aged, or old. (See Pifer & Bronte, 1986.)

It is unfortunate also that outmoded stereotypes of aging and old age still prevail. To counter some of those stereotypes, the second part of this chapter presents basic data about the economic, social, and health status of older people. Such data need to be examined if we are to understand how well older people are faring in the United States today.

The third part addresses five major policy issues that are now in the forefront of public awareness and that illustrate ways in which concerns about the aging society often distort our ideas about policy problems. These issues are often perceived to relate more to the welfare of older persons than to the welfare of others, but in all five instances, the issues have relevance for the entire society. The discussion should also make clear that although major policy questions are being reshaped by the changing age distribution, they are not themselves outcomes of that change.

The Aging Society

The term *the aging society* denotes the changing age distribution of the population, in which the proportion of old to young is rapidly increasing. At the turn of this century, 1 of every 25 persons in the United States was age 65 or older. Today it is about 1 in every 8. And by the year 2020, when the baby boom will have become the senior boom, it is expected to be 1 in every 6, or even 1 in every 5. This trend marks a revolutionary change in human history.

There are two reasons for this dramatic change. One is the low birthrates of the past few decades, rates that are expected to continue to be low in the decades ahead. Many families are choosing to have fewer children, due partly to the changes in women's roles, partly to increased education and affluence whereby parents no longer consider children as necessary sources of financial support, and partly to advances in contraception that provide reliable methods of controlling both the planning and prevention of pregnancies.

The second reason for the changing age distribution is that people are living much longer today. At the turn of the century, the average infant born in the United States was expected to live to age 47. Today that figure is 75.[1] Even more striking is the fact that when Americans reach age 65, they can now expect to live another 17 years, to age 82. Average life

---

Bernice Neugarten presented a Master Lecture at the 1988 APA Convention. The lecture was based on this chapter, which was produced in collaboration with Neugarten's daughter, Dail A. Neugarten. Dail Neugarten is an associate professor in the Graduate School of Public Affairs, University of Colorado at Denver and executive director of the National Leadership Institute on Aging, in Denver.

[1] This fact and other statistical facts given in this chapter are drawn from data presented in *Aging America: Trends and Projections* (1987–1988 ed.), a source book prepared by the U.S. Senate Special Committee on Aging (1988), in conjunction with the American Association of Retired Persons, the Federal Council on the Aging, and the U.S. Administration on Aging. For each set of data, the original source is cited in that source book. In most cases, the source is the U.S. Bureau of the Census, the National Center for Health Statistics, or another government agency.

expectancy is often regarded as the best single index of a society's quality of life—one that reflects the biomedical, social, educational, and economic factors that, taken together, produce the level of physical and social health of the population.

Gains in life expectancy have occurred because of the conquest of most infectious diseases and, within the past few decades, because of new medical treatments for chronic conditions. Medical interventions that reduce hypertension and that prevent or treat coronary disease are notable examples of advances in overcoming chronic illnesses. In addition, certain changes in life-styles, such as changes in diet and smoking habits, appear to be adding to average life expectancy.

Longevity is, of course, not synonymous with good health. It is not altogether clear what greater longevity will mean in the future with regard to the health status of older people as a group. The evidence is clear that the vigorous and active part of the life span has been lengthening, and in that sense we have been producing a 20th-century version of the Fountain of Youth. But advanced old age may mean, for many individuals, slow failures in one body organ after another. Science and medicine may continue to develop palliative means that prolong rather than shorten the duration of terminal illnesses. In different words, medical advances may keep people alive but may not keep them healthy or happy.

At present, it is clear that more and more people are surviving into the oldest age group, where the need for supportive services is greatest, especially the need for long-term care. For the immediate future, this group will remain a small proportion of persons over 65; but as the numbers multiply, it is the population over age 85 that will be of greatest concern to health planners and other policymakers.

All the developed countries of the world today are aging societies, although they vary somewhat in terms of average length of life. Even in the developing countries, where average life expectancy is much lower, the number of persons over 65 is expected to grow dramatically over the next few decades, barring famines, the uncontrolled spread of AIDS, and other catastrophes. The aging society is therefore a worldwide trend, and it is expected to continue well into the future.

The Specter of an Aging Society

Some persons, when they first give attention to the changing age distribution, are greatly troubled and think of the aging society as disastrous. They are concerned about how the economy will support increasingly large numbers of retirees who are viewed as a nonproductive drain on society. Or they wonder how the society will provide for older persons who are frail, disadvantaged, and in need of special care. Or they want to know how the health system, which is presently focused on high-technology medicine and on the cure for acute illness, can become a system geared to care rather than cure. Some are concerned that national government expenditures for older people are about as high as the expenditures for national defense (nearly 30 percent of the annual budget), and that if current trends continue, this percentage will continue to climb. Still others wonder what conflicts among age groups might arise.

Some think about possible "fixes" for the aging society. Could the population be better balanced by increasing the birthrate, perhaps by providing incentives to women to bear more children? This type of intervention has not proved successful in those European societies that have tried it, for instance, by offering "family grants" for each child born; nor is it likely to succeed in the United States. This is because we cannot turn back the changes in family structure and in women's roles. The movement of women into the labor market has brought with it new educational, economic, and social opportunities for women, as well as higher levels of economic well-being for their families. Therefore, encouraging women to stay at home and have more babies is not likely to be a successful policy.

There are other observers who have thought about rebalancing the age distribution by developing humane ways of ending people's lives when they grow too old, such as withholding life-prolonging medical treatment from very old, very sick persons (Callahan, 1987). It may be true that some forms of medical treatment are burdensome and unwelcome to some old patients, or that they may only be ways of prolonging the process of dying. Still, the proposal to withhold medical treatment from very old as opposed to younger patients offends the ethical and religious principles of many persons. For some, it violates the sense of responsibility they feel for the welfare of their own aged parents, or it raises the issue of what medical care options they will have when they themselves grow old. It is not likely that such a proposal will meet with consensus in a society like our own that has such diverse social, ethical, and religious values.

Thus, such "fixes" are not likely to work. The aging society is here to stay, demographers tell us, even after the baby boomers become the senior boomers and have passed through the population pipeline. The growth in numbers of older people in the United States will be slower, but there still will be growth.

The specter of an aging society that will collapse under the burden of its elderly members needs closer examination, however. The first question is how well older people are faring in today's society and what the implications may be for future older people. Is there cause to worry? Is there more cause than is warranted by the evidence?

How Well Are Older Persons Faring?

Our best knowledge today is that persons grow old in widely diverse ways. There is no single pattern of social, psychological, or biological aging—

given, of course, that people are born, grow up, and die, and that in postindustrial societies, most people grow old before they die. There are differences between persons, between the sexes, between racial and ethnic groups, and especially between socioeconomic groups. It should come as no surprise that people age differently, yet it was a surprise to the many who believed the stereotype that lingering illness, poverty, decline, and constriction characterize the lives of all people as they grow old.

The reality is that despite wide variations in life histories, most old people, until they reach what is known as the *oldest-old* period of their lives, are in relatively good health, have at least modest levels of income, and appear to be well integrated into their families and communities. (See *Milbank Memorial Fund Quarterly*, 1985.)

Health Status

Although age is not a good predictor of health status for any given individual, it is a powerful predictor of rates of illness in groups of individuals. On the basis of probability, the older a person is, the greater the vulnerability and the greater the risk of disease or impairment. It is well known that the increased frequencies of illness in older persons are in chronic rather than in acute conditions. Arthritis, hypertensive disease, hearing impairments, and heart conditions are the most frequently occurring health problems. In persons over 65, the large majority report at least one chronic illness, and in a large proportion, it is not one but several chronic conditions that are present simultaneously (U.S. Department of Health and Human Services, 1989. See also Committee on an Aging Society, Institute of Medicine of the National Research Council, 1985.).

But reported illness and impairment do not necessarily result in disability. It is not the presence of particular diseases but the number and severity of functional disabilities that are the preferred measures of health status. Persons consider themselves in ill health primarily when an illness or impairment interferes with their activities of daily living, which are defined as personal care and home management or home maintenance tasks. The data show that, as might well be anticipated, such health-related difficulties increase with advancing age. Yet it is noteworthy that of persons aged 65 to 74, over 80 percent report no limitations in carrying out these daily activities. For the next oldest age group, those 75 to 84, more than 70 percent report no such limitations. And even for those over age 85, who constitute the oldest one percent of the population, half report no limitations.

It is important also that persons with severe disabilities, including those who are unable to care for themselves, represent a relatively small proportion of all older persons (about 17 percent of all those aged 65 and over). Most of these persons are, once again, in the very oldest group.

We should not underestimate the problems of those who are significantly burdened by ill health and those who are dependent on others for their day-to-day care. These are the men and women who not only require but receive by far the greatest amount of care from their families and from both medical and social service agencies in the community. We merely point out that, at present, the large majority of older people are in quite good health and only a minority are ill or disabled.

Economic Status

The ways that people age and their quality of life once they grow old are closely related to the economic health of the society at large. In the decades after World War II, but especially since the early 1970s, the economic situation of older people as a group has greatly improved. As have other developed countries, we have created in the United States a three-part system of economic support for retirees and their spouses that rests on public and private pensions and, much less than before, on personal savings. The system supports persons in some cases as long as 30 years after retirement, a result of the fact that people are retiring earlier but living longer.

The large majority of older persons are not poor, although the range in income is very wide. The number of older men who have very high incomes is about the same as the number who live in poverty.

The picture is somewhat different for women, of whom a much larger proportion have incomes near or under the poverty line. (In 1987 some 15 percent of women over 65 lived in poverty, compared to 9 percent of men over 65.) This discrepancy is related to the fact that the majority of women over 65 are widowed and were in the labor force only intermittently; as a consequence, they have meager or no Social Security benefits of their own. Very old widowed and never-married women are particularly disadvantaged in this respect.

Minority-group older people, especially Blacks, also have very low economic status. In these groups, the social and economic disadvantages that have accumulated throughout their lives are accentuated in old age.

On average, older persons have substantially lower cash incomes than do younger people. At the same time, they have certain economic advantages, such as government in-kind transfers not available to younger persons (primarily health care costs covered by Medicare), and lifetime accumulations of assets (primarily the equity in their own homes). Some analysts contend that when such factors are taken into account, the average older person has economic resources roughly equivalent to those of an average person of working age. Using the poverty line again as a marker, there are about the same proportions of older adults as younger adults who have very limited economic resources. For men and women together, 12 percent of persons aged 65 and over lived below the poverty level in 1987, compared with 11 percent of persons aged 18 to 64.

Social Participation and Attitudes

Older people appear to be faring relatively well also according to other indices. Again, there are large differences between individuals and between subgroups, but the stereotype that old people are lonely and isolated does not fit today's reality any more than the stereotype that they are ill and poor. The large majority report active family ties, close friends whom they see frequently, good relations with neighbors, and participation in churches and synagogues. Seventy-five percent of the men are married and living with their spouses. Among women, however, more than half are widowed by age 65, and half are living alone by age 75. In a recent survey, about half of those older persons with children reported seeing one of their children within the previous day; a majority reported giving help when a child or grandchild was ill; and one fourth reported giving financial assistance to a child within the previous year (Louis Harris and Associates, Inc., 1981).

Most older persons "grow old in place"; that is, they remain in the same communities, often in the same houses they have occupied for most of their adult lives. (For the first time, in 1980, more older people lived in suburbs than in cities.) About 75 percent own their own homes, and about 80 percent of those homes are mortgage-free.

It is significant that the vast majority of persons retire before age 65 and begin to take Social Security benefits at 62 or 63. (Only 16 percent of men and 7 percent of women over 65 are presently in the labor force, over half of whom work only part-time.) They retire, not because they are "put on the shelf" by their employers, but because they decide they have enough income to withdraw from the labor force. They spend their time in various ways, with a majority reporting that they spend considerable time socializing with friends. Others are involved in recreation and hobbies, and more than one in five do regular volunteer work. It is probably relevant in this connection also that with national educational levels rising over the past few decades, more than half the persons who were 65 and over in 1987 had completed high school, and about 10 percent had four or more years of college.

Most older people report high levels of life satisfaction. Compared with younger adults, about the same high proportions hold positive self-images and feel that life is better than they had anticipated. Only a small minority of older persons, fewer than 20 percent—about the same proportion as among young people—report that loneliness is a serious problem.

Young-Old and Old-Old Populations

Another way to portray how older people are faring is to describe them according to whether they are *young-old* or *old-old* (B. L. Neugarten, 1974. See also B. L. Neugarten & D. A. Neugarten, 1986.). This distinction, based not on age but on health and social characteristics, cuts across the wide range of differences among older people. The young-old group is the large majority. These are the vigorous and competent men and women who have reduced their time investments in work or homemaking, are relatively comfortable financially and relatively well educated, and are well-integrated members of their families and communities. It is estimated that young-old persons comprise 80 to 85 percent of all persons over 65. Seeking meaningful ways to use their time, many serve their communities in remunerated or nonremunerated ways. They represent a great pool of expertise and talent to the society, talent that is increasingly recognized and utilized. (See Committee on an Aging Society, 1986.)

The old-old group, by contrast, consists of those who suffer major physical, mental, or social losses and who require a range of supportive and restorative health and social services. Essentially these are persons who are in need of special care. Some live in institutional settings, but most remain in the community. Because their illness and frailty levels are extreme, the needs of these persons preoccupy policymakers at both the local and national levels.

The major conclusion to be drawn from these kinds of data is that old age itself does not define a problem group in today's society. Some older people are economically and socially needy; most are not. By most socioeconomic measures, it is a small minority who are severely disadvantaged. These are mainly very old persons, who, compared with those born later, have been disadvantaged earlier in their lives with regard to education, occupational skills, medical care, and pension systems.

All in all, drawing upon the best data available, we can conclude that as a group older persons appear to be faring well, surely much better than their parents or grandparents, and in many ways as well as other adult age groups. These conclusions are significant departures from traditional stereotypes, and they are important in the formulation and implementation of public policies.[2]

---

[2] Douglas W. Nelson (1982), in the chapter entitled "Alternative Images of Old Age as the Bases for Policy," describes three alternative frameworks for policy making, each based on a different view of the status of older persons: the first, that age should be irrelevant in meeting the needs of adults; second, that old age should be redefined and the marker moved up to age 75; and third, that old age should be treated as an earned status like veteranship and that older persons should accordingly be given special rewards. Nelson spells out the policy implications of each of these views.

Policy Issues in an Aging Society

The aging society and the status of older persons in this society have direct impact on the policy issues that have confronted us over time. From among such issues, five have been selected here to provide examples of varying specificity: first, the state of the economy, and in relation to it, the viability of the Social Security system; second, the provision of health care, particularly the problem of cost containment; third, the problem of eldercare; fourth, the mobility and safety of drivers and pedestrians; and fifth, what has been called the issue of generational equity. None of these issues are new, but all have become refocused because of the changing age distribution. What is important is that these issues, along with many others, have neither been created by the aging society nor should they be discussed in the framework of outmoded stereotypes of older persons. They are complex policy concerns around which comlex policy decisions must continue to be made. The aging society is only one of the lenses, albeit an important one, through which they should be viewed.

The State of the Economy

Our economy is changing dramatically, from an industrial to a service economy and from one focused on manufacturing goods to one focused on producing information. It is increasingly reliant on technological innovations that demand high levels of education and skill. Public goods and public services are proliferating, and they are being provided by new cooperative delivery arrangements and new public–private partnerships.

The work force is changing as well. More women are working, and the number of part-time workers is increasing rapidly. Women and older workers, most of whom are neither unionized nor covered by pension systems, make up a large share. People are entering the labor market later, and as already mentioned, they are retiring earlier. The lengthening of education and the lowering age of retirement are occurring in all industrialized countries of the world.

Many people are concerned about the capacity of the economy to maintain our relatively high standard of living for the population at large. The federal deficit, our international trade imbalance, declining capital investments, international competition, and the lowered productivity of the American worker are valid issues to worry about. But the one that relates directly to our aging society is the concern that our economy cannot bear the burden of so many older persons, who by reason of their age alone are considered consumers but not producers. This issue is often described in terms of the so-called dependency ratio, usually expressed as the number of older people (aged 65 and over) to the number of working-age people (aged 18 to 64). The presumption is that everyone in the older group can be considered a nonproducer and therefore dependent, whereas everybody in the younger group is a producer. This logic is faulty. Not all persons aged 65 and over are nonworkers and not all persons aged 18 to 64 are workers; in fact, sizable numbers of people in their 20s, 30s and 40s are not. A dramatic change over the past decade has occurred in the age group 55 to 64, in which only 3 out of 5 men are now in the work force. Thus, the dependency ratio does not reflect the reality of who is an economic producer and who is not.

If a dependency ratio is to be used at all, it should include both old people and children as dependents. This inclusion is important, because if the birthrate continues to stay low (as it is predicted to do) and if young people (under age 18) are included in the ratio, we have little cause for alarm. Workers should continue to be able to support the nonworkers because the drop in the numbers of children will more than offset the rise in the numbers of old persons. In the 1960s, if both children and older people are counted in, the ratio was 83 dependents to 100 persons of working age. This was at the height of the baby boom. By 2030, the height of the senior boom, this ratio is projected to be only 75 to 100.

If the relative size of age groups per se is not important, we might think instead about the relative numbers of those who are and are not actually in the labor force. But even that index is too broad. For example, in the United States today, fewer than two percent of male workers are engaged in agriculture, yet agricultural production remains very high. So the size of the labor force is also an unsatisfactory measure of the country's productivity.

Economists use productivity per worker as the index of the society's economic health. Productivity, in turn, depends on three major factors: first, the amount and utilization of capital available to workers; second, the educational and skill level of workers; and third, the factors we lump together and call technology. Thus, when we look at the health of the economy, even through the lens of an aging society, we should do better than to worry about the proportion of old people to young people. Although it cannot be undertaken here, what is needed in assessing the state of the economy is an economic analysis, not merely a demographic one. (See Palmer & Gould, 1986.)

The Social Security system. The question about the economic viability of an aging society is often focused more directly on the Social Security system and whether it can support increasing numbers of older people, especially the baby boomers when they reach retirement age. This concern is also exaggerated because the Social Security system is constantly being adjusted to the changing demography and the changing economic circumstances of both older and younger persons. These adjustments have been the rule in the past and will continue into the future.

The Social Security program was created in 1935 as one of the major government programs for helping the country recover from the Great Depression. It was intended to replace the income lost by older persons, almost all of whom were unemployed and unlikely to reenter the labor force. It was therefore an important step in keeping older persons from poverty. (See Achenbaum, 1986.)

The system has always been a flow-through or pay-as-you-go system, which means that approximately the same amounts of revenue come in from the taxes paid by workers as are paid out to older persons who are the beneficiaries. (A small part of the revenue is set aside for unexpected contingencies.) Social Security is usually described as the federal governent's single most successful program. Its benefits have gone steadily up; it is administered efficiently; it is regarded as equitable and fair; and it has the strong support of the public. One major index of its success is that today, without it, the 12 percent of older persons who live in poverty would grow rapidly to 50 percent.

In the present context the important point is that the system is continually changing in terms of the dollars paid in and the benefits paid out. Every few years, Congress passes amendments to readjust the tax and benefit levels. Complex economic and demographic projections are made in figuring out ways that income and expenditures can be kept in balance. For example, the 1983 amendments to the Social Security Act, in recognition of the upcoming baby-boom generation and vast future needs, established levels of intake and outgo whereby the system is now building vast surpluses. The system is constantly monitored by its own board of trustees, which makes regular reports to Congress and to the public.

In short, the Social Security system is a carefully crafted and carefully watched program. There is no reason to believe that the balancing and rebalancing will not continue into the future. No modern society could maintain itself if a large proportion of its adult population had no regular source of income, either through their own or through spouses' work, or through some system of public pensions.

The real issue before us, then, is not that the Social Security system cannot support the aged people in an aging society. It is rather that we need to keep educating the public, especially young people, about the way the system operates. As a system, Social Security is not in jeopardy. The health of our economy and the success of our Social Security system will depend upon factors other than the proportion of young people to old people.

Health Care

An aging society brings with it various problems related to health care. At present, escalating health care costs are causing the most public concern. Many factors contribute to the rise in costs, a rise which if measured by total national health expenditures, equals 600 percent in the last 15 years. These factors include general inflation, the rapid escalation of physician fees, the mushrooming costs of hospital care, and the increasing use of expensive high-technology medicine. Health care is now 11 percent of the gross national product—a percentage that most observers regard as too high, although others regard it as too low.

Another factor contributing to escalating health care costs is the increasing number of older people. No one quarrels with the fact that, as an age group, older people have more illnesses than younger people and greater needs for health care, despite the fact that they report their health as relatively good. Older men and women see physicians more frequently, are hospitalized more often, and have longer stays in the hospital. Similarly, it is acknowledged that approximately one third of the total health bill for the country is for the care of persons 65 and over, who constitute only 12 percent of the population.

All this is reflected in Medicare, the program that provides health care insurance to persons over 65 under the Social Security system. (It is worth noting that the United States is the only industrialized country that provides health insurance only to older people rather than to the population at large and the only industrialized country that is presently without a national health care system.)

Medicare is not the only public program that provides coverage to older people. Medicaid, the program that provides health care to persons of all ages who are poor (persons usually referred to as medically indigent), also contributes a large part of its budget to persons over 65, especially in covering costs of nursing-home care.

The Medicare expenditures, however, provide the most useful index for measuring the effects of the aging society, not only because it is the largest share of all health expenditures for older people, but because it is now a large proportion of the federal budget and therefore very visible to the public. Medicare expenditures multiplied elevenfold during the years from 1970 to 1986, compared with the sixfold increase in total health expenditures for the population at large.[3] It is important to note that a small proportion of older people, about 17 percent, account for over 60 percent of Medicare payments. This statistic confirms the fact that while the age group as a whole uses a high proportion of all medical services, it is only a small fraction of that group who are actually responsible for the high usage and thus for most of the high cost. It also supports the

---

[3] Health expenditures are usually expressed in current dollars that are not corrected for inflation. But when corrected for inflation, total health care expenditures for the United States in the 17-year period from 1970 to 1987 multiplied by nearly two and a half times. In the same period, expenditures for Medicare multiplied by almost four times.

conclusion that most old people are not very sick, at least not until the last year of their lives.

Older people themselves still pay about one third of their total health costs, despite both Medicare and Medicaid, and they pay more dollars out of pocket today than ever before. Accordingly, older persons, like younger ones, are directly affected by the other health cost factors mentioned earlier: the rise in physician and hospital costs, inflation, and the increasing use of high-technology medicine. Medical economists point out that the aging factor, although it is important, is only one of the factors driving health care costs and one that by no means matches the others in significance.

Here again, then, we frame the problem incorrectly for the society at large if we frame it as an outcome of the changing age distribution. The aging society brings with it increased health care needs and health care expenditures, but our ability to provide quality care that is cost-effective depends on many factors other than the fact that the proportion of older people is rising.

Health care costs are not, of course, the only problem with our health care system. With the conquest of most infectious diseases, it is chronic, not acute, care that is the major need. Yet the medical system is still based on the "cure" rather than the "care" model.

Chronic illness is long-term, often lifelong, and it requires long-term, if not life-term, management. Chronic illness follows a course in which there is usually an acute period that may require hospitalization, followed by a longer period of remission, and in which this pattern repeats. The patient becomes the manager of his or her own care and knows when certain kinds of social and medical services are required. Physician and hospital services become the auxiliary, rather than the central, component of treatment.

The patient's home, rather than the hospital, becomes the center of management. And in a home-based system, a new type of cooperative relationship between doctors, nurses, patients, family members, and other service providers must be developed. Health care personnel need to be trained and ready to provide home services and to share authority with the patient, perhaps to yield it over the long haul (Strauss, 1987. See also Corbin & Strauss, 1988; and *Quality Health Care: Critical Issues Before the Nation*, 1988.).

Chronicity, of course, is not a new problem, but the growing numbers of older people are bringing into sharper focus the need for a newly conceptualized health care system, one that is more focused on the problem now called *long-term care*. Long-term care requires both social and medical services, and often if patients could receive more of the former, they would need less of the latter.

We must not overlook the fact that long-term care needs have been growing for young persons as well as for old. Severely disabled infants are now being kept alive who, in earlier decades, could not have survived.

And rates of disability in persons of working age also have increased rapidly, as shown by the numbers who receive benefits under the disability provisions of the Social Security Act. Once again, then, even though the aging society has brought a problem into sharp focus, the problems of health care—whether related to costs, location, or quality—are problems for the whole society and not outcomes of the fact that the society is aging.

Eldercare

An issue that relates to long-term health care but that arises more directly from the aging society is the issue of *eldercare*—the physical and emotional caretaking of older members of the family, whether that care is day-to-day physical assistance or the responsibility for arranging and overseeing such care. Most old people live in the community, either in their own homes or in the homes of their children, usually the homes of their daughters. Eighty percent of all health care provided for older people is given by the family.

Historically, the family's primary responsibility for its elders was financial; but since that responsibility has been largely shifted to the government by the creation of the Social Security system, the family's primary responsibility is now physical and emotional caretaking of older family members.

With the increased numbers of four- and five-generation families, it is not unusual for middle-aged persons to have two generations above them. It is probably the first time in history tht a woman can be a granddaughter and a grandmother simultaneously. (See Hagestad, 1986.) One of the accompanying realities is that a large number of women now have family responsibilities for most of their adult lives. Some are caring for as many as four or more older people, and some are caring for parents and children (and sometimes grandchildren) at the same time. The problem is not only one for women, although women are usually the providers of daily physical care. Many men also report that a major life stress is their concern that their parents receive adequate care.

The major issue relative to eldercare is how it will be appropriately provided. With so many women in the labor market, who will replace them as caregivers? There is the added problem that many caregivers are in their 60s (some of whom are themselves ill), who find it especially stressful to be caring for relatives who are in their 80s.

There is a burgeoning literature on eldercare and the need to provide supports to caregivers. Some observers are advocating that government provide financial support to families to help provide home services or to substitute for the loss of income if a worker reduces outside employment to care for an aging relative. Others are proposing systematic programs of respite care. Some large business organizations are helping workers with parent-caring, for example, by providing flexible work schedules and creating more part-time or at-home jobs. Government supports have been slow to appear. A major reason is that many persons in the society believe that such government interventions will weaken the family's responsibility and therefore have a deleterious effect on the well-being of older, as well as younger, people.

Other persons are more appropriately viewing the problem of elder-care as only one part of the broader problem of caregiving, that is, as already mentioned, the problem not only of providing care for old persons but also for young persons. There is a growing recognition, too, that caregiving is a responsibility also of the community at large and that new forms of cooperation must be negotiated between families and formal and informal community agencies. (See Brody, 1985.)

Mental health care. In any discussion of caregiving, mental health support for older persons is an important issue. We should not underrate the importance of providing emotional support to caregivers; as the society ages, however, the supply of mental health services for older persons themselves becomes a compelling problem.

The problem is growing because of the increasing number of persons in the very oldest group, the group most at risk of developing both organic and affective mental disorders. It is widely recognized that all potentially disabling physical conditions have emotional and behavioral components, and emotional supports become central in the care of most medically ill people. The system of mental health services is beginning to recognize the needs of elderly persons, but, unfortunately, mental health services for older persons are sparse. For instance, only half of the more than 600 publicly supported community mental health centers have services designed specifically for older people. And psychologists, psychiatrists, and social workers in private practice see very few older persons. Some observers estimate that by the year 2000, the numbers of professionals (psychologists, psychiatrists, other physicians, social workers, and nurses) who are specifically prepared to provide health and social services to older people will need to be increased by 50 percent in each category.

Again, the policy question that the aging society is bringing into sharper focus is how to provide appropriate mental health services for the recipients of eldercare as well as for those who provide it.

The Built Environment and Transportation

Another set of issues relates to needed improvements in what is called the *built environment.* The term refers not only to the immediate environment of the home but also to the neighborhood, where safety and accessibility to shopping and personal services are important. It includes also the transportation system: public transportation, roadways, and personal automobiles. In short, the term describes the wide array of elements that are the province of architects, developers, and city planners.

One pressing need related to the built environment is in the area of transportation, where the question is how to make both streets and automobiles safer for all drivers and pedestrians. One of the organizations concerned with this issue is the Transportation Research Board (an arm of the National Academy of Sciences), which has recently completed a two-year study focused on older drivers and pedestrians. Its findings illustrate how improvements made for older persons could improve the quality of life for everyone. (See Transportation Research Board, 1988; see also Committee on an Aging Society, 1988.)

Mobility is essential to older as well as to younger persons. Given the inadequacy of public transportation systems and given the high proportion of older persons who live in the suburbs, older people (like younger ones) are increasingly dependent on the automobile, and increasing numbers of older people (especially women) are drivers. According to the Transportation Research Board, more than 80 percent of all trips by people over 65 are made in automobiles, and that rate is increasing.

Although most older drivers have good driving records, accident rates among older drivers (even though they are not as high as those among the youngest drivers) are disproportionately high. Because older persons drive far fewer miles than do younger persons, the meaningful rates are those calculated on the basis of number of miles driven. On this basis, there is a sharply rising accident rate after age 75 and a higher rate of involvement in fatal crashes.

In general, vision, hearing, and speed of reflexes involved in driving tasks diminish with age. At the same time, for any given individual, age is a poor predictor of driving performance. In recognition of the latter fact, state licensing agencies usually require drivers who are in their late 70s and beyond to be more frequently tested for driving performance than younger drivers, but they do not withhold licenses on the basis of age alone.

The Transportation Research Board suggested a whole range of improvements for automobiles and roadways that would reduce traffic accidents and fatalities. These include respacing the headlights on cars, redesigning traffic intersections, improving roadway markings and signs, and reviewing licensing procedures for all drivers. One interesting recommendation was to reexamine the time intervals for walking across intersections; in many places the traffic signals are timed according to the normal walking speed for college-age men but are too fast for most older pedestrians.

It is obvious that as improvements are made in the transportation system, benefits will accrue to drivers and pedestrians of all ages. This is an excellent example of how policy interventions aimed at benefiting older persons are ways of improving the quality of life for everyone.

Generational Equity

The final policy issue we will discuss here is taken from the political arena. It is the so-called generational equity issue, misnamed because the meaning intended by the most concerned people is generational *inequity*. This concept suggests that our aging society is being unfair to younger people because we are piling up advantages for older people in the allocation of our national resources. This argument further contends that such unfairness produces conflict among generations (or, more strictly speaking, among age groups) and therefore produces divisiveness in the society at large.[4]

This is another instance where there is more smoke than fire, for there is no systematic evidence that age–group conflicts are increasing.

The issue is usually posed in terms of people of working age versus retired people. It is said, for example, that workers are protesting the rise in Social Security taxes. Yet repeated national surveys show very stable support in the public at large for Social Security and for Medicare. The most recent public opinion data show that adults of all ages, including the young, are not only strongly in favor of the Social Security system but are also willing to pay higher taxes to support it (Cook & Barrett, 1988. See also Yankelovich, Skelly, and White, Inc., 1985.). One of the major reasons for this attitude, of course, is that most adults prefer a strong Social Security system to the alternative of putting the financial responsibility for older people back on the family. They realize that a public policy that benefits older people is one that benefits most younger people as well.

One of the organizations concerned about the equity issue, Americans for Generational Equity (AGE), has stated the issue somewhat differently. They claim that today's baby boomers, now in their 30s and 40s, will find when they grow old that the Social Security system will not pay out at the same rate it pays present retirees or that it will not be there at all. We have already commented on the security of the Social Security system and need not repeat those comments here.

It is a curious argument that AGE is making for another reason, however. Today's baby boomers constitute a very large part of the voting population and will continue to do so. Will they not be the people, as they grow old, who will cast their votes and produce, from their own ranks, the policymakers who will be framing national policies and programs? Will the baby boomers, highly educated and articulate, merely stand by helplessly and allow the system to fail them?

---

[4] There is a wide range of views regarding the so-called generational equity issue. For two of the most clearly opposed, see the book by Longman (1987), which sets forth the Americans for Generational Equity (AGE) position, and the book by Kingson, Hirshorn, and Corman (1986).

Before leaving the topic, let us note that the generational equity issue sometimes takes form by raising the question of whether the "advantaged old" population is using up resources that should go to disadvantaged children. Old people are advantaged in this view because they have publicly provided pensions (Old Age Survivors Insurance, often called Social Security), health care (Medicare), and other benefits that other age groups do not have. Older people have greatly benefited as well from federal programs such as food stamps, housing subsidies, and tax advantages. They have benefited, too, from the growth of private pensions and government regulation of private pension funds.

While this trend has been occurring, the numbers of children living in poverty have been rapidly increasing. The numbers are presently over 20 percent of all children as a group, and about 40 percent of Hispanic and Black children. Most poor children are found in single-family homes, homes usually headed by women, of whom a sizable proportion rely on public assistance. (This situation is a big part of the problem of "feminization of poverty" in the United States).

It is undeniable that the large number of poor children is a disgrace in our affluent society. But the question of how we should deal with the problem is misstated when the number of poor children is compared only with the number of more affluent adults. The problem should not be viewed as an intergenerational equity issue but as a major shortcoming of our broader economic and social policies. One way in which the poverty problem regarding children is being attacked is the recent congressional legislation that is a partial reform of the welfare system. The legislation provides job training for welfare mothers so that they can move into independent private-sector jobs, and it provides for child care while these mothers are being trained.

This legislation is only one step that may prove effective. It is widely recognized that we need many policy approaches in dealing with poverty. The problem of today's poor children is part of a larger and more complex set of issues, namely, the question of how to determine what proportion of federal resources should go to social programs and how to allocate those resources to the various groups who need assistance. To refer to such issues as generational equity does not help our understanding; it only gives a catchy journalistic term for a complex set of problems.

Conclusion

As these and other policy issues are debated, we should keep in mind that underlying any effective policy interventions in our aging society must be a change in our attitudes about aging and its implications for social and psychological functioning. Some of the negative stereotypes about aging are disappearing; one that persists, however, and that could be particularly damaging to the aging society is that older people lose their curiosity, creativity, and ability to learn, and that because they are not able to adapt to new ideas, they stand in the way of innovations and social change. As a result, according to this reasoning, our aging society will inevitably decline socially, intellectually, and culturally.

The realities that counter this stereotype are many. One, mentioned at various points in this chapter, is that older people are decidedly heterogeneous. Indeed, they are more different from one another than are younger people by almost any economic, social, or psychological measure. The metaphor of a fan is useful here: the longer that people live, the more they fan out. Some are sick and disabled by the time they reach 60; others maintain their leadership in business, government, and academia well into their 80s; and some do their best creative and artistic work when they are in their 90s.

Another important fact discussed earlier is that most older people are faring well. Most are young-old and are physically, intellectually, and socially competent. Still another reality is that patterns of aging are changing. People today age differently from the ways people aged 50 years ago, and they will age differently 50 years from now. We do not yet know the limits of change, but we know that a wide range of positive interventions can continue to be made in the lives of older people, just as they can for younger people. The major contribution of both biological and social scientists in the past two decades has been that they have changed the climate of opinion about aging and that we have a far more constructive view today than the one that prevailed earlier.

We have learned that from knowing only the age of a person we cannot predict his or her behaviors, competencies, or needs. Similarly, from knowing only the age distribution of a society, we cannot predict how that society will function, what challenges and opportunities will arise, and what its accomplishments will be.

We have become aware that a focus on the aging society should not divert us from dealing squarely with the social problems endemic to a modern society. Economic viability depends in some measure on providing income maintenance for all those who need it. Quality health care that is cost-effective is necessary for poor people as well as for rich people. Caregiving for those young, middle-aged, or old who need it is an important determinant of the quality of life for the community at large as well as for the individuals most directly affected. Good physical environments and good transportation services are essential for people of all ages. And the just and equitable allocation of resources to all groups in the society is the important social goal.

Finally, we have learned also that as people live increasingly long lives, a society that adapts to that fact may become an "enabling" society for both young and older people. An aging society is not a specter that should frighten us. We would do better to think what the spirit of our aging society might become and to what extent it might be a beneficent spirit that could assure a range of options for people of all ages.

Bibliography

Achenbaum, W. A. (1986). *Social Security: Visions and revisions.* New York: Cambridge University Press.

Brody, E. M. (1985). Parent care as a normative family stress. *Gerontologist, 25,* 19–29.

Callahan, D. (1987). *Setting limits.* New York: Simon and Schuster.

Committee on an Aging Society, Institute of Medicine/National Research Council. (1985). *America's aging: Health in an older society.* Washington, DC: National Academy Press.

Committee on an Aging Society, Institute of Medicine/National Research Council. (1986). *America's aging: Productive roles in an older society.* Washington, DC: National Academy Press.

Committee on an Aging Society, Institute of Medicine/National Research Council. (1988). *America's aging: The social and built environment in an older society.* Washington, DC: National Academy Press.

Cook, F. L., & Barrett, E. J. (1988). Public support for Social Security. *Journal of Aging Studies, 2,* 339–356.

Corbin, J., & Strauss, A. (1988). *Unending work and care: Managing chronic illness at home.* San Francisco: Jossey-Bass.

Hagestad, G. O. (1986). The family: Women and grandparents as kin-keepers. In A. Pifer & L. Bronte (Eds.), *Our aging society: Paradox and promise* (pp. 141–160). New York: W. W. Norton.

Kingson, E. R., Hirshorn, B. A., & Corman, J. M. (1986). *Ties that bind: The interdependence of generations.* Washington, DC: Gerontological Society of America.

Longman, P. (1987). *Born to pay: The new politics of aging in America.* Boston: Houghton Mifflin.

Louis Harris and Associates, Inc. (1981). *Aging in the eighties: America in transition.* Washington, DC: National Council on Aging.

Milbank Memorial Fund Quarterly: Health and Society, 63 (1985).

Nelson, D. W. (1982). Alternative images of old age as the bases for policy. In B. L. Neugarten (Ed.), *Age or need? Public policies for older people* (pp. 131–169). Beverly Hills: Sage Publications.

Neugarten, B. L. (1974). Age groups in American society and the rise of the young old. *Annals of the American Academy of Political and Social Science, 415,* 187–198.

Neugarten, B. L., & Neugarten, D. A. (1986). Changing meanings of age in the aging society. In A. Pifer & L. Bronte (Eds.), *Our aging society: Paradox and promise* (pp. 33–51). New York: W. W. Norton.

Palmer, J. L., & Gould, S. G. (1986). Economic consequences of population aging. In A. Pifer & L. Bronte (Eds.), *Our aging society: Paradox and promise* (pp. 367–390). New York: W. W. Norton.

Pifer, A., & Bronte, L. (Eds.). (1986). *Our aging society: Paradox and promise.* New York: W. W. Norton.

Quality health care: Critical issues before the nation. (1988, March). Washington, DC: Health Care Quality Alliance.

Strauss, A. (1987, November/December). Health policy and chronic illness. *Society*, pp. 34–39.

Transportation Research Board, National Research Council. (1988). *Transportation in an aging society: Improving mobility and safety for older persons* (Special Report No. 218). Washington, DC: National Academy Press.

U.S. Department of Health and Human Services. (1989). *Health USA, 1988*. Hyattsville, MD: U.S. Government Printing Office.

U.S. Senate Special Committee on Aging. (1988). *Aging America: Trends and projections* (1987–1988 ed.). Washington, DC: U.S. Government Printing Office.

Yankelovich, Skelly, and White, Inc. (1985). *A fifty-year report card on the Social Security system: The attitudes of the American public*. Washington, DC: American Association of Retired Persons.